THE BACK DOCTOR
TELLS YOU:

- What causes the three major types of back pain, and how you can determine your own type

- Why there is no such thing as a "slipped" disc or a back "going out"

- How stress affects your back

- How "imaginary" pain can be all too real

- How you can relieve sudden pain—no matter where you are or when it occurs

- Why severe pain does not mean serious disease—and surgery is usually not the answer

THE
BACK DOCTOR
HAMILTON HALL, M.D.

TEN MINUTES A DAY TO LIFETIME RELIEF FOR YOUR ACHING BACK

BERKLEY BOOKS, NEW YORK

This book is not intended to replace the services of a physician. Any application of the recommendations set forth in the following pages is at the reader's discretion and sole risk.

This Berkley book contains the complete
text of the original hardcover edition.
It has been completely reset in a type face
designed for easy reading, and was printed
from new film.

THE BACK DOCTOR

A Berkley Book / published by arrangement with
McGraw-Hill Book Company

PRINTING HISTORY
McGraw-Hill edition / September 1980
Berkley edition / April 1982

ISBN: 0-425-05307-5

Contents

Illustrations

Introduction

One evening not long ago, I was waiting to deliver some after-dinner remarks on the nature of back pain to an audience concerned with accident prevention. I found myself seated at the head table next to an expert in industrial safety.

My dinner companion wasn't a doctor but he had acquired a good deal of knowledge about industrial back injuries. He told me that he had heard me speak before and had enjoyed my comments on the misconceptions many people have about their backs. But he was curious about some of my remarks.

"You aren't going to tell them there's no such thing as a slipped disc?" he asked.

I replied that I would.

"But," he said, "don't you get into trouble with your colleagues, going around saying things like that?"

At that moment I realized that this safety expert was harboring his own misconception — that I was a squealer on my own profession, a sort of medical stool pigeon who was revealing secret truths about the human back.

I explained that, far from getting into trouble with my colleagues, I was simply telling the public some of the things that doctors have known and agreed on for years. Certainly there is no conspiracy of silence. But for various reasons — the pressure of time, an inability to communicate in plain language, and, in a few instances, a lack of sensitivity — some doctors fail to give their back patients the information they need.

I know I would have welcomed any information

about back pain when I became a victim of backache at age seventeen. My pain was triggered by construction work during a summer job. It didn't occur to me to see a doctor. I just assumed that it was a normal part of my initiation into the construction crew to spend several weeks walking around hunched forward like a monkey, eyes fixed on my safety boots. Since then, however, I have taken some consolation from the realization that at least I was never subjected to the misinformation some backache sufferers have heard, or think they've heard, from other doctors.

I happen to believe that, whatever the ailment, every mature patient is entitled to full and accurate information from his physician. But with backache there is special need for straightforward communication. Knowledge and understanding are the best means of dispelling unwarranted fears and creating the self-confidence that is essential in dealing with a bad back.

With that aim in view, I have always made a point of explaining the facts of common backache to my patients. For several years I conveyed the message, as most doctors do, to one patient at a time. Then I realized that I could save their time and mine, and perhaps do a more thorough job of informing them, if I presented the material more systematically to small groups of patients. Initially, this was nothing more than an attempt to communicate some important, though rather mundane, information in a simple and convenient way. Yet it was soon obvious that these group sessions were filling a definite need that must exist among many back patients besides my own. And so, in response to patient demand, those early sessions initiated at Women's College Hospital, Toronto, in May 1974 grew to be an organization now known as the Canadian Back Education Units, which today operates classes for backache victims in twenty communities, with branches throughout Ontario and affiliates in Quebec, Alberta, Michigan, Kentucky, Arizona, Ohio, Florida, and even Perth, Australia.

Although the patients who attend our classes every year number in the thousands, they represent only a small fraction of all backache victims. This book has been designed to reach that larger population of men and women who, regardless of where they live, can benefit from a program that has been practised with proven success for over five years.

In gathering the material presented here I have drawn on the knowledge and experience of my colleagues at the Back Education Units. The preparation of the text owes much to the skills of Hal Tennant, whose assistance is here gratefully acknowledged. My thanks are due also to Margot Mackay for her care in the preparation of the illustrations.

As you will see, this is not merely an exercise book, nor is it strictly a how-to or self-help manual in the conventional mold. Those elements are present in these pages, but the message runs deeper than that. It is my hope that, as a typical victim of common backache, you will arrive at the final page of this book with a sense of encouraging self-confidence, a new-found ability to take charge of your own body, and a clear awareness that the basic responsibility for making your back better rests with you.

As a backache sufferer, you may have been told at some time that you must learn to live with your pain. I don't believe that's necessary — not when I can show you, instead, how to learn to live with your back.

Hamilton Hall, M.D., F.R.C.S. (C)
Toronto
April 1980

1 The Things a Back Doctor Hears

Every year, several thousand men and women parade through my office, one by one, complaining of back pain. That in itself is hardly surprising. As an orthopedic surgeon — a bone-and-joint doctor — I specialize in helping people with back problems. And, like most people who work hard at a subject they know, I've had my share of successes.

The remarkable thing about my work, though, is the amount of time I have to spend educating people about their own spines. Don't misunderstand me. My patients are intelligent people. In most respects, including the fact that they suffer from back pain, they're quite typical of the population at large. But, also typically, they have absorbed an appalling amount of misinformation about the human back. After listening to these people talk about their backs, day after day, year after year, I am convinced that no other part of the human body — not the brain, not the sex organs, not even the heart with all its symbolic mystique — has given rise to so many misconceptions, so much silly folklore, and so many unwarranted fears.

I've discovered that the human back is regarded as such an enigma that people confronted with back problems often abandon all common sense and whatever knowledge they do possess of physiology. They apply peculiar tests and rules they would never dream of applying to other parts of their bodies.

It's all so self-defeating.

There is such a thing, of course, as harmless superstition, even when it applies to your back. Remember that old rhyme we used to recite as kids whenever we walked along a concrete sidewalk? "Step on a crack — break your mother's back!" Some of the commonest beliefs adults have about their backs are just as absurd as that children's rhyme. But they are far from harmless. Misinformation encourages countless numbers of people to behave self-destructively. They endure back pain unnecessarily. They undergo treatments and exercises that are needlessly painful and in some cases useless. And meanwhile they forgo many satisfying activities — golf, gardening, or sex — that they could be enjoying.

If that description fits your situation, this book is meant for you. It will tell you the things I tell my patients, and more — everything you need to know about your back: how it's put together, how it works, why it sometimes becomes painful, and how you can control or even eliminate that pain.

It is important, first of all, to rid yourself of any false notions you may have about your back. Let's begin by looking at the beliefs I hear voiced, day after day, by new patients.

"The human back is a very special part of the body."
Certainly your back is special in the sense that it's important. But so are your brain, your heart, your liver, and many of your other organs. Your back is not unique. In fact its parts are remarkably similar to those found elsewhere in your body: its bones have an internal structure like a honeycomb — just as your heel bones have. It has small joints that are like the joints in your fingers. Its discs are quite similar to a joint you have in the front of your pelvis. Its muscles are much like the muscles in your thighs. Its ligaments resemble the ligaments in your ankles. Even the tunnel in each vertebra, through which your spinal cord passes, isn't all that different from the openings in the backs of your eye sockets, through which the optic nerves enter the brain.

* * *

"My back is an inexplicable piece of anatomy with problems so complex they are impossible to diagnose."

If you happen to share that belief, I'd like to ask you why. Is your back a mystery to you because you can't get a good look at it? Or does it frighten you because it has parts with strange names like cervical vertebrae and sacrum and coccyx? Perhaps you are bewildered by diagrams you've seen of the human back, with its confusing array of bones and muscles and ligaments and nerves. Or did a doctor alarm you by saying he wasn't sure what was causing your pain?

Suppose I told you that I own a mysterious and complex machine called an automobile. It has thousands of parts, including many I've never seen. A lot of those parts have strange names — like carburetor and cylinder head and alternator. Could I convince you, on the evidence, that this mysterious machine of mine is capable of breakdowns that can baffle the best minds in the automotive world?

Hardly. You would rightly point out that whatever might go wrong with my car, all I need is either a skilled mechanic or a good repair manual and the right tools. You might agree that the repairs could be expensive and time-consuming. But you would continue to insist that my "mystery machine" couldn't possibly be too complicated for diagnosis by a competent repairman.

Neither is your back.

"My back is one of the most fragile parts of my body."

Do you think so? Let me tell you about an airline accident that proved just the opposite.

At eight o'clock on the morning of Monday, June 26, 1978, Air Canada Flight 189, a DC-9 jetliner bound for Winnipeg, began its takeoff from Toronto International Airport. Flight 189 never got off the ground. As it reached a speed of 120 miles an hour, the plane skidded off the runway and plunged fifty feet into a ravine. Fifty feet is a long drop, equivalent to driving your car off the roof of a five-story building.

The DC-9 carried 107 people — passengers and crew. All were wearing lap belts. As the plane hit the bottom of the ravine, they were thrown violently forward. The impact of the crash was estimated later at 20 to 30 g's — four to five times the gravitational force astronauts experience during a launching. Pinned into place by the belts around their mid-sections, the plane's occupants were literally folded in half. The strain on their backs was tremendous. Yet fewer than half the people aboard that plane suffered back injuries. Make no mistake about it, this was a serious accident. Two passengers died (though not from spinal injuries) and many others, subjected to an enormous force while restrained by their seat belts, suffered serious injuries to their backs. My point, however, is that in spite of those forces, the majority of the people aboard survived without back injuries of any kind. If our backs were as fragile as many of my patients suppose, nobody could have come away from Flight 189 without serious spinal damage.

Or consider the case of the apprehensive adulterer. Mr. X became a patient of mine immediately after undergoing a disastrous and terrifying experience. He had developed a passion for a certain woman who, unfortunately for him, was married to someone else. One night, the classic confrontation occurred. The amorous couple were discovered together in her sixth-floor apartment. Whether Mr. X jumped or was pushed I never learned, but, either way, he tumbled from the sixth-floor balcony, landing on his feet on the roof of a neighboring two-story house. You can imagine how the impact was transmitted up through his body. When I examined him in the emergency ward, I found Mr. X had broken both heels and both legs, and had suffered various internal and head injuries. And yet there was nothing wrong with his spine.

* * *

"I've been told I have a slipped disc. Can you put it back into place for me?"

You may find this hard to believe, but there is no such thing as a slipped disc.

I know you've heard the expression dozens of times, and even your own doctor may have used it. If so, he didn't intend to convey the impression it gave you. Most people know they have discs between their vertebrae. They imagine a disc to be something like a poker chip — thin, hard, and slippery, and thus capable of popping easily out of position. When this happens, they think they need a professional — a chiropractor, a physiotherapist, or a doctor like me — to pop it back into place for them. In reality, discs never slip out of place. They bulge.

We'll be going into more detail about discs in a later chapter, but for the moment forget about the poker-chip image. Think, instead, of a tap washer — that little rubber doughnut that seals off the flow of water in a faucet. If you've ever changed a washer, you will have noticed that when you fasten it down tight, the washer bulges slightly. That's roughly what happens whenever there's pressure on a disc in your spine. When a disc bulges far enough to come into contact with a nerve — an uncommon occurrence, incidentally — the condition is often referred to as a slipped disc. But I think it's a pity the term ever came into use, and I wish people, especially doctors, would stop using it. It conjures up an image that is false and frightening.

"I could tell the instant my back went out — I heard it crack."

Like the slipped disc, the notion of a person's back "going out" is part of modern folklore. Comedian George Burns, always ready with a gag based on his advancing years, once declared: "At my age, my back goes out more often than I do." When someone tells me his back has "gone out," the expression makes me want to ask, "Where does it go? Does it stay out all night, or does it come tiptoeing back in around 2 a.m. with some lame excuse about having to sit up with a sick friend?"

Just as it is erroneous to describe a disc as having "slipped," it is wrong to describe a spine as having "gone out." It is true that under certain conditions you may hear a cracking sound in your spine. That sound is the same as the one that is heard when a person cracks his or her knuckles. In the joints of your fingers and in your spinal joints you have nitrogen in solution, under pressure. If you pull suddenly on your finger, you decrease the pressure on the joint. This causes the nitrogen to come out of solution and turn temporarily from liquid to gas in much the same way that champagne goes "pop" when you uncork the bottle. Now, to many people, the act of cracking the knuckles is as offensive as belching at the dinner table. But it's not harmful. And just as nobody ever pulled a finger off while cracking his knuckles, nobody ever "threw his back out," even though it may have sounded like it.

If you hear a cracking sound when you're having your spine manipulated by a physiotherapist or a chiropractor, you may believe that one or several vertebrae have been snapped back into place. But the truth is that your back has never really been "out." If, after it makes a cracking sound, you suffer pain or experience relief, there are other reasons why.

"My back hurts. Do you suppose it's arthritis?"

Could be. But that doesn't explain what's causing the pain. The first syllable of "arthritis" comes from the Greek word for "joint." The suffix "-itis" means an inflammation, which is a condition, not a disease. Arthritis, then, is simply an inflamed joint. Suppose you noticed that I had an inflamed eye — what is commonly called a bloodshot eye. You would realize instantly that it was a condition, not a disease in itself, and you might ask whether it was the result of an accident or an illness, or perhaps evidence of a hangover. What you might not realize is that I could also suffer an inflamed or "bloodshot" condition in almost any joint of my body. I could get a "bloodshot" or inflamed toe joint by stubbing my toe while walking barefoot on a rocky beach. Or I might get the same condition in one of my spinal joints as a result of an accident, disease, or — commonest of all — plain, old-fashioned wear and tear. Wherever my inflamed joint might be located, it would properly be referred to as arthritis. Once you understand that arthritis is a condition that could have any one of several causes, you realize there is no such thing as a single cure for it. More important, you appreciate the fact that arthritis, as a word, is really nothing to fear. And, as a condition, it may be no more serious than a bloodshot eye or a stubbed toe.

"I don't dare work in the garden (play tennis, have sex) for fear of injuring my back."

I must say I sympathize with people who feel that way. What they should understand, however, is that there is an important difference between pain and injury. Tending your tulips may pain your back, but it won't cause injury. As we've already seen, your back can stand a lot of abuse without suffering actual damage. Often you'll feel pain simply because you are using muscles in some unaccustomed way, or pushing them beyond their normal limits. To test this principle for yourself, try the following experiment. Pick up a heavy book and hold it in one hand at arm's length. Within a few minutes your arm muscles will begin to complain. Later the pain will become intense. And yet you won't damage your arm. At the most, you'll have sore arm muscles for a while. But so what? We've all experienced muscular soreness — from painting a ceiling, or wheeling topsoil for the lawn, or riding horseback, especially if it's for the first time. Without suffering bruises or other injuries, we incur pain, either at the time or later, or both.

The same principle applies to your back, even if it has been sore in the past. No normal activities, such as lobbing a tennis ball, swinging a golf club, or mowing the lawn, will damage your back. But they may cause pain. It may be more than muscular pain; it may even be acute and severe pain resulting from stress on your spinal joints or discs. But it won't cause damage. And only you can decide whether the activity provides enjoyment that's worth the price of the pain.

Whenever you choose to endure a certain amount of pain in return for a pleasurable experience, you're making a trade-off. I will have more to say about trade-offs in a later chapter. Meanwhile, start getting used to the idea that even an acutely painful activity won't damage your back. "Hurt" is not the same as "harm."

"I don't remember ever injuring my back, but I must have or it wouldn't be hurting — right?"

This notion is especially popular with people who pride themselves on not knowing their own strength (although you could argue that it's a matter of not knowing their own weakness). If you ever became roaring drunk, you might do some quite damaging things to your body without realizing it at the time. But, otherwise, it's most unlikely that you could strain yourself enough to cause serious injury without being aware of it. No sensible person would accept the idea of being able to suffer a broken leg or a dislocated elbow without realizing until much later that some serious damage had occurred. Yet many people are willing to believe that the equivalent injury could happen to their spines without their knowing it.

Such is the mystique of the human back. And, like several other popular myths, it ignores the commonest cause of back pain: the ordinary wear and tear that is a normal part of living and growing older.

* * *

"It's an old childhood injury, but it hasn't bothered me for years — until now."

Not long ago, a woman of twenty-eight came to see me about a pain in her back. She had already decided what had caused her problem. At the age of five she fell off a porch and hurt her back. I asked her how often she'd had back pain during the twenty-three years since her accident. "Never," she said, "until just last week."

This "childhood injury" theory has no basis in medical experience, and yet I can understand why people are ready to believe it. If you have back pain, it's natural to assume you've been injured. Most people try to pin down the "when" and the "how." They have no trouble dredging up a recollection of some plausible-sounding incident. All of us have had childhood accidents or misadventures that seemed, and perhaps were, quite serious at the time: a fall off a bicycle or a garage roof; an accident in a too-shallow swimming pool; a bodily collision on a playing field. If an old injury has bothered you, off and on, for years, then it may in fact have some relationship to a present pain. But there is no such thing as a serious bone or joint injury lying dormant for years and then suddenly flaring up. That may seem to have happened to your back, but in reality your present pain must have some other cause.

"It must be really serious — the pain is unbearable."

Here's another fact you may find hard to believe: there is little relationship between the seriousness of a back problem and the amount of pain it causes. Some serious ailments cause only mild pain. Conversely, you can suffer severe pain from a short-lived condition that is no threat to your health. The condition called wry neck is a good example. Wry neck is a form of muscle spasm that can cause excruciating pain to shoot up and down your neck with the slightest turning of your head. Yet it causes no damage, it's usually gone in a few days, and it may never recur.

"It's bad enough having the pain in my back, but I'm afraid it will spread to the rest of my body and leave me paralyzed."

That would be a terrifying prospect if it were real. Perhaps you are among those who imagine your back problem to be an insidious disease that is coursing up and down your spine, threatening to spread to your arms and legs. Fortunately, that isn't what back pain is all about. Most back conditions cause some pain to be relayed into the legs. But the cause of your pain is almost certain to be located in one small part of your spine, probably in a disc or in one of the small joints we call facet (rhymes with cassette) joints. In all likelihood it's a mechanical problem, comparable to a worn or damaged link in a chain. As long as it's weak or damaged, the pain will persist and place a little extra strain on nearby discs and joints. But it won't spread like some contagious disease. On the contrary, with proper care and exercise, it will probably repair itself, and the pain will go away.

"I'm only thirty-six and my back is so bad already I'm sure it will deteriorate by the time I'm sixty."

Your prospects are probably much better than you think. Statistically, back pain is less frequent in old age. I often compare a patient's spine to a machine, to illustrate how wear can impair efficient function. But, unlike an old car, your back has the capability of repairing itself, and evidently this is what happens to the majority of people who have common backache during middle age. A Swedish study carried out in the late 1960s indicated that backache is at its peak of incidence between the ages of thirty and sixty. In 1979, the Canadian Back Education Unit studied 3,500 patients and reached a similar conclusion — that the incidence of backache was greatest between the ages of forty and fifty-nine. Of course, there's no guarantee that you will be among those who benefit from natural mending, but the statistics are definitely on your side. This, incidentally, is one reason why backache is such an economic and social problem: it strikes more often during people's working years, not after retirement.

The natural healing process takes years and is accompanied by joint stiffness and loss of height. Certainly a sixty-year-old doesn't have the spinal flexibility of a teenager. But, typically, the back pain is gone and the spine has retained enough strength and movement to satisfy the most active senior citizen. In a recent back education class I found that two of the participants were mother and daughter — a woman in her sixties and her mother, who was eighty-five. The daughter was there because she had a back problem. Her mother just came along for company. "I used to have back trouble when I was her age," the mother explained, "but now it's all better."

I am not suggesting that back pain is unknown in old age. Some elderly people do suffer from it. But they are a minority, and their backs are rarely afflicted by the mechanical conditions I am discussing throughout this book. In elderly people, backache is more often related to bony spurs on the vertebrae (which occur when Nature overdoes the repair process) or to primary diseases of the bone, such as osteoporosis, which makes the vertebrae readily vulnerable to fractures. (These and other rarer causes of backache are described in Chapter Five.)

"My husband says I'm just imagining the pain, and I'm beginning to wonder if he's right."

All pain is real. If you feel pain, there is pain. You are not "just imagining the whole thing." But it is also true that your emotions can add to your discomfort or even bring on an attack of pain. Once you have experienced back pain, it is impossible not to have an emotional response to it. The very fact that you dread and fear it can make the pain worse than it would otherwise be.

Your emotions can also cause a pain attack, through their relationship with body tension. We all know that when we experience certain emotions, the muscles in our bodies become tense. That happens to all of us whether we have back problems or not; in moments of stress, our muscles tighten up, especially in our necks and our backs. If you happen to have a worn joint in your spine, the muscular tension that is associated with emotion may produce pressure on that joint and actually produce pain.

Whichever way your emotions may be related to your back pain, it's incorrect and unfair to suggest that "it's just your imagination."

"My back will always be painful until I find exactly the right mattress (office chair, car seat)."

Unlike most misconceptions I hear from my patients, this one usually develops after the person has learned a bit about back care, such as the best positions for standing, sitting, and sleeping. According to the old expression, a little learning can be a dangerous thing; but I've found that with back patients it's usually just boring or silly.

One of my patients is a man who brings his car-seat problem into my office. We go over it together. Should it be tilted five degrees or only three? I try to tell him he ought to arrange it in whatever way is most comfortable. But that's not enough for him: he always insists on pinning me down to an exact number. So I may tell him to make it six and a half degrees or fourteen degrees, depending on the mood I happen to be in that morning.

Mr. Car Seat is forever buying and selling cars, always according to his current notion of seat comfort. Whatever make or model he has chosen, he jams magazines under the driver's seat. He believes that, as his back doctor, I should decide whether he's likely to be more comfortable with *Time* or with *Playboy*.

Obviously the man is obsessed. But I can't tell him the whole thing is a figment of his imagination. Instead, I let him go through his routine. If he announces this week that an eight-degree tilt and three copies of *Sports Illustrated* under the seat are just right, I say, "Fine."

Who am I to argue? Having reviewed the latest literature in my field, I can tell you that medical science has yet to come up with the perfect car seat, the perfect office chair, or the perfect mattress. Some chairs and mattresses are better than others, but what's perfect for one person may be uncomfortable for another. And in any event, what you sit on or sleep on is far less important than the *way* you sit and the *way* you lie when you sleep. I hope, some day, to get that point across to Mr. Car Seat.

If my back problem is serious, I expect I'll have to undergo surgery."

To almost every back patient I see, I explain two basic points about surgery. One is that fewer than five percent of all people with back pain are likely to benefit from surgery. At least nineteen out of twenty, including serious cases, are better off with some combination of physiotherapy, medication, exercise, and what we refer to as proper ADL — activities of daily living; that is, the proper positions when standing, sitting, lying in bed, and so on.

The second point is that surgery is no magic solution to any back problem. If the problem is located in one specific spot, if it is diagnosed properly, and if it does not respond to other forms of treatment — all these ifs are important — then surgery may put an end to your pain. But if the pain is originating from more than one point in your spine, or if the problem is not structural in nature, no surgeon can provide a solution with one swift, neat operation. He can't operate on pain; there must be a specific physical condition that can be corrected or improved by surgery.

When I have a patient who does need surgery, I always emphasize two other points, both of which follow from what I've just said. The first is that no matter how successful the operation is, your back will never be normal again; surgery creates scar tissue which doesn't exist in a normal back. My second point is that even the most successful surgical operation is just one of several steps necessary to control the problem. If you are to undergo surgery, you must be prepared to make permanent changes in your life-style after the operation, doing the exercises and adopting the daily postural habits that will maintain your back in good condition, free of pain.

"Other people may have back problems, but mine is unique."

We all like to think we're special. Ordinary ailments are for ordinary people. It nurtures our egos to believe that whatever ailment we have is rare in the annals of medicine. Without actually saying so, most of my patients feel that if they have to be ill, then, dammit, they're going to suffer from something unusual and dramatic.

I was given a vivid demonstration of this phenomenon not long ago by a group of twenty-five people, all of whom had back pain. At the time I spoke to them, these people already knew that the three commonest causes of back pain are disc trouble, wear and tear of a facet joint, and a pinched nerve. They also knew that of those three causes, the pinched nerve is the least common, occurring in only about one case out of every ten. I asked the members of this group to tell me, by a show of hands, which of these causes they believed was responsible for their own back pain.

Put yourself in their place. How much sympathy could you expect if you announced at your next cocktail party, "My doctor says I have wear and tear on a facet joint"? Can't you just see people's eyes beginning to glaze over already? Now try this one:

"Did you ever have a pinched nerve in your spine? Well, I have. . . ." Now there's a medical drama for you. It feels painful just to describe it.

By now you can guess how that group of twenty-five people responded to my question. Even knowing how low the statistical chances were, every man and woman in that room thought that he or she had a pinched nerve. I knew otherwise. I had examined them all, one by one, and none of them had a pinched nerve. They had all simply picked the cause they considered the most spectacular.

"I've been to five other doctors with this problem, and not one of them told me what you have just been telling me now."

That may be true. But often a doctor tries to explain a back problem without managing to get his message across. Some doctors don't take the necessary time to explain. Others find it hard to express themselves without using a lot of medical jargon that their patients don't understand. Even when the doctor spells out the whole thing in plain English, the patient may be too bewildered or too fearful to absorb and remember the information.

I don't pretend to be a genius at doctor-patient communications. But I work at it. And I try to make sure my patients understand everything they ought to know about their backs — what's wrong and what needs to be done to make it right. Even so, I find myself dealing with patients at moments when they are too upset to appreciate what I'm telling them.

That's one reason why I believe this book should be helpful. A lot of the information here might not actually be new to you, but it may seem new simply because you can consider it calmly and appreciate it more readily than when you heard it from your doctor. Even if it seems familiar, it will reinforce what you already know and enlarge your understanding of your problem.

As you read through the chapters that follow, I hope you will adopt the techniques I suggest for preventing common back pain. I hope you will acquire the self-confidence and ability to cope with any attack you cannot prevent. And I wish you the satisfaction of accepting trade-offs by which you tolerate some pain in exchange for the enjoyment of a favorite activity you once avoided.

Most of all, I hope that the information in the rest of this book will help you substitute knowledge for any fear you now feel towards your back pain and its cause. For, in eliminating that fear, you will eliminate much of the pain itself.

2 Bogeyman, Ping-Pong, and Other Diversions

How do people with back problems manage to pick up so much harmful information?

I can think of many ways. They listen to old wives' tales. They diagnose themselves incorrectly and exchange their erroneous findings with their friends. They misquote articles they've read. And in some instances, sad to say, they can cite their own doctors as the sources of their false notions and unwarranted fears.

There's a double irony here. For one thing, doctors are supposedly reliable sources of medical information and advice. Second is the fact that few patients of any kind are more in need of clear and accurate information, both general and specific, than those who suffer from back pain.

Yet there are general practitioners and even orthopedic surgeons who speak loosely of "slipped discs" and backs that have "gone out," even though they know better. And there are family doctors, and specialists too, who avoid talking frankly to their patients and resort instead to evasion, innuendo, and incomprehensible jargon.

Why do some doctors behave this way?

In many instances, I'm sure, it's purely unintentional — simply a matter of their being less sensitive or less adept at interpersonal communication than they might be. In other instances, I believe, they resort to game-playing because they feel uneasy and unsure of themselves when confronted with back patients and their problems. Often their discomfort is obvious, even to laymen. Once, at a social gathering, I met a man who said he derived great satisfaction from taking his wife around to see doctor after doctor about her bad back. He explained that he hated medical people, and "I like to watch a doctor sweat."

Many family doctors are uneasy with back pain because they find it tricky to diagnose and unsatisfying to treat. Some specialists, on the other hand, find it a bore. To the surgeon whose life revolves around the operating table, back patients are chronic complainers whose conditions neither appeal to his mentality nor challenge his well-honed skills. A back problem cannot be diagnosed precisely the way, say, a fractured wrist can. The treatment a back needs will likely be non-surgical. The improvement it shows, if any, will likely be slow and undramatic. And a cure is out of the question. All in all, the doctor who is dedicated exclusively to surgery sees back treatment as a thankless and unrewarding task.

Although I don't share that view, I can understand and even condone it. The conduct that results, however, is something else, since it has a seriously detrimental effect on many patients who deserve better. Such effects are evident among some of the people who visit the office and clinic where I practise.

If you have ever gone to a doctor to complain of back pain, you may recognize yourself as the patient in one, or several, of the following games.

Speaking Doctor

In my private life, I speak English, just as most of my patients do. In my professional life, however, I communicate with my colleagues in medical jargon — a language I call Doctor. Like the jargon of other occupations, Doctor has its place. But it doesn't belong in a doctor-patient consultation, such as this one:

* * *

PATIENT: Doctor, I have something wrong with my neck.
DOCTOR (examining): You have cervical spondylosis.
PATIENT (recoiling): Oh, my God!

What did the doctor actually say here? He used the term "cervical spondylosis." If the patient had had a Doctor-English dictionary at hand, she could have discovered that "cervical" refers to the neck, "spondyl" indicates the spine, and "-osis" means "disease of" or, more loosely, "something wrong with." Hence, "cervical spondylosis" is simply Doctor for "something wrong with (the spinal portion of) your neck."

When the exchange is rendered entirely in English, it comes out in this improbable form:

PATIENT: Doctor, I have something wrong with my neck.
DOCTOR (examining): You have something wrong with your neck.
PATIENT (recoiling): Oh, my God!

As you might suppose, this game can be played with any Doctor term referring to any part of the body; for example:

PATIENT: Doctor, look at this rash on my skin.
DOCTOR: Ah, a case of dermatosis! (Derma = skin; -osis = disorder.)
PATIENT: And I thought it was only a rash!

As you can see, the Doctor language has the power among laymen to make even the most mundane diagnosis sound terribly profound, medically learned — and frightening. That's not really why doctors use it. They learn to speak Doctor in medical school because they can't practise medicine without it. By the time they graduate, they've been exposed to 50,000 words of Doctor. And it's invaluable to them. It has precision. It's concise. And it's universally understood within the medical community.

A few doctors may speak Doctor to their patients to mask their own diagnostic weaknesses, but I believe the trouble usually begins when the doctor forgets that his patients understand only a few terms —words like appendicitis and tonsillectomy. Without intending to bewilder or frighten anyone, he may lapse completely into Doctor, using many expressions known only to medical people. Ironically, at that moment, he may be attempting to allay the patient's fears, as in, "This is only a contusion." Those are not necessarily reassuring words to someone who doesn't realize that a contusion is just a bruise.

The game of Speaking Doctor is especially unfortunate when it's played with back patients, because their treatment depends for its success on their thorough understanding of what's causing their pain, what they can do about it, and why they needn't be afraid of it. If your doctor uses a term you don't understand, ask for a translation, and don't be intimidated by those ten-dollar words.

But even plain English, imprudently used, can frighten a back patient, as we see in this next game.

Bogeyman

In half a century of film-making, the creators of horror movies have proved that audiences can be frightened most by the unknown. We all react with greater terror when the Thing is still on the other side of the door. We've all watched horror movies where the monster's appearance was a letdown because its unseen presence beforehand was far scarier.

The underlying principle, of course, is simple: nothing we are told or shown is as frightening as what we can concoct in our own imaginations. The game I call

Bogeyman is based on this principle, which, again, is often evoked unintentionally by doctors when they say things they don't really mean, or when they imply more than they intend to. Either way, there are usually four elements in this game, with only the first element — the doctor's statement — spoken aloud. The other elements consist of what the Bogeyman whispers to the patient, what the doctor actually meant, and what the patient needed to hear at that moment for his own information or reassurance.

In a general practitioner's office it might go this way:

THE DOCTOR SAYS:
I don't know what's causing your pain.

THE BOGEYMAN WHISPERS:
In other words, you have a mysterious disease — cancer maybe!

THE DOCTOR MEANT:
I know ordinary back pain when I see it, but in your case I can't pinpoint the exact cause or source.

THE PATIENT NEEDED TO HEAR:
I can't determine the exact source of your pain, but that's not important at the moment. The first thing to do is to get a few days' bed rest, which will probably make the pain go away.

In a surgeon's office, a Bogeyman game might be played this way:

THE DOCTOR SAYS:
I'm afraid I can't help you.

THE BOGEYMAN WHISPERS:
He's telling you you're a hopeless case!

THE DOCTOR MEANT:
I'm a surgeon — and you don't need surgery.

THE PATIENT NEEDED TO HEAR:
You don't need surgery. In fact, even though your condition is very painful, it's not serious.

Some surgeons have the unfortunate habit of disowning patients who don't need surgery — which, in the case of back patients, is the vast majority. One surgeon I know likes to tell his patients, "I'm a cutting doctor, not a talking doctor." To me, that seems like the ultimate rejection of doctor-patient communication. But at least that surgeon leaves patients knowing where they stand. In contrast, the doctors who play Bogeyman arouse groundless fears that help perpetuate the false mystique of back pain.

Mum's the Word

This is a variation of Bogeyman. In this version of the game, the doctor simply leaves vital information unsaid by ignoring the patient's questions.

THE PATIENT ASKS:
Is there something seriously wrong with my spine?

THE DOCTOR (preoccupied) RESPONDS:
Did you ever have a bad fall?

THE BOGEYMAN WHISPERS:
He knows something! He's just groping for some way to break the bad news!

THE DOCTOR MEANT:
It's too early to tell, but while I'm examining you I might as well get a few extra facts.

THE PATIENT NEEDED TO HEAR:
There's no reason to think it's serious. Do you know that most people have back pain like this at some time in their lives?

Double Diagnosis

Two or more doctors can play. Each player takes a turn examining the same patient. All players must reach the same conclusion (diagnosis) but each must express it in entirely different terms. Object: maximum patient confusion. In its simplest form, Double Diagnosis is played this way:

PATIENT: What's wrong with my back, Dr. Smith?
DR. SMITH: You have facet arthritis.
SAME PATIENT (one month later): What's wrong with my back, Dr. Jones?
DR. JONES: You have spinal osteoarthrosis.

Dr. Smith and Dr. Jones are not disagreeing. Dr. Smith is saying that the patient has spinal joints that are inflamed. Dr. Jones is saying that there is something wrong with one or more of the patient's spinal joints. The only difference is that Dr. Jones's loftier phrase may cost the patient eight dollars more.

Even at that, this patient was relatively lucky, since only two doctors were playing. I knew a woman with a broken ankle who got into a game of Quadruple Diagnosis. She went to four doctors who all agreed on what was wrong. The trouble was, nobody told her they agreed. From Doctor One she learned she had a spiral fracture. Doctor Two said it was an oblique break of the lower tibia. The third doctor called it a transverse crack with displacement. And the fourth labelled it Pott's Fracture.

There were no contradictions here. Spiral, oblique, and transverse merely describe the direction of the break in the bone. Pott was the first man to describe this type of fracture. The four doctors were simply stating the same problem in different terms, or seeing it from different points of view — a phenomenon that is not peculiar to medicine.

The confusion created by Double Diagnosis is compounded by certain patients. These are the neurotic "doctor shoppers" who see physician after physician as they search for the diagnosis they want to hear.

Crystal Ball

I know of doctors who warn their patients, "I wonder if you realize what will happen to your spine if you don't undergo this operation. . . ." And then they go on to predict some dire consequence, such as a lifetime of pain or disability, or both.

A doctor who makes a prediction like that is playing the game I call Crystal Ball. In my view, it's risky and unfair. The risk to the doctor's credibility is obvious. We've all heard stories about people who were told, "You'll never walk again," and who now, years later, are walking around as ably as ever and sneering at their doctors. Crystal Ball is especially risky with back patients because most bad backs get better without drastic treatment of any kind.

Why would a doctor utter such predictions? Usually, he's trying to coerce a patient to submit to a treatment he believes is right in the circumstances. But even if the prediction comes to pass, such tactics exert unfair pressure on the patient. I believe every mature patient has the right to hear a full and truthful description of any treatment and its risks and consequences before deciding whether to accept it. Perhaps your doctor has been making flat declarations about your future condition, suggesting that you will suffer unpleasant consequences unless you take this treatment or that. If so, my advice is to seek a second opinion. No good doctor will object.

I have also known doctors who play Crystal Ball not to talk a patient into an operation but to get rid of him. In this variation of the game, the doctor implies that an operation is really the only feasible remedy, but then he goes on to paint a lurid picture of how the operation could go wrong. That puts the patient in a bind — unwilling to risk the operation yet unable to get better without it. At this point the patient usually looks for help elsewhere — which is just what the doctor wanted. But imagine the problem of persuading this patient to accept back surgery, should it really become necessary at some time in the future.

Thou Shalt Not

This game might also be called "Oh, You Helpless Cripple!" It's based on the premise that once you have back pain you might as well throw in the towel (but throw it very gently). No more fun for you. It's time to learn a list of "don'ts" as long as your arm — and remember: you ignore even one of them at your peril!

A back specialist I know hands his patients a list of Thou Shalt Nots that is so forbidding that it always reminds me of Alexander Woollcott's famous complaint that everything he liked was either illegal, immoral, or fattening. While the Bible manages with only Ten Commandments for all mankind, my colleague needs twice that number of Shalt Nots to control his back patients' behavior. And that's just his general list; there are supplementary strictures as well for housewives engaged in vacuuming, sweeping, kitchen chores, laundry work, stair-climbing, and bed-making.

What's more, many of his rules are so impractical that they are laughable: "Don't reach." "Never lift anything weighing more than fifteen pounds." "Don't get tired." How can anybody observe rules like those and still get on with the process of everyday living? Back patients need guidance, but in my opinion it's worse to have too many rules than to have no rules at all. A person faced with a ridiculous prohibition like "Don't reach" is unlikely to pay attention even to the reasonable rules on the list.

I was given a first-hand lesson in Thou Shalt Not

long before I entered the medical profession. In m
mid-teens I'd been having a little trouble with m
sinuses, and so at my parents' urging I went to
doctor. He declared that the only way to clear up m
condition was to avoid sweaty situations — no heav
physical exertion, no steamy showers, no humi
locker-rooms. Now, I had just made the high schoo
football team, and here was a doctor telling me, i
effect, Thou Shalt Not Behave Like a Football Player
Can you picture a young man following that advic
just to clear up a bit of sinus trouble? Hardly. I simpl
ignored what he said and made sure my parents neve
found out. My sinuses, by the way, are fine.

Why do doctors dispense such unrealistic advice
Some, I think, naively believe that patients will giv
up comfortable habits and familiar pleasures just t
feel better. And of course they won't, any more than
was willing to give up football. In other instances
especially with back cases, I think doctors issue Shal
Nots because they can't think of anything else to do
But, worst of all, I believe some doctors use rule
making as a means of building an escape clause int
their advice. After all, if a doctor's rules are numerous
enough and stringent enough, some are sure to be
broken sooner or later. Then, if the patient's pain
recurs, guess who is left feeling guilty. Certainly no
the doctor.

Ping-Pong

The most popular game on our list, Ping-Pong, will
seem familiar to almost any reader who has been
seeing back doctors for six months or more. Ping-pong
is described here in more detail than the other games
because lengthy duration and endless variations in
diagnosis and treatment are the very essence of the
game. A good game of Ping-Pong can last for months,
even years.

Any number of doctors and paramedics can play,

nd the more players there are, the more devastating
he game. The object is to bat the patient back and
orth as many times as possible before he realizes that
e is the ping-pong ball.

In our play-by-play example below, the players are
family doctor (who gets an assist from a colleague on
he opening serve), plus a physiotherapist, an ortho-
edic surgeon, and a psychiatrist. Their ping-pong
all is Charlie, forty-seven, a chartered accountant.

Readers who are aficionados of Ping-Pong are in-
ited to take particular notice of the finesse of the
rthopedic surgeon, who, at the first moment the ball
s on his side of the net, manages to play, in rapid
uccession, five of the six other games described
arlier. Indeed, the opportunity to introduce one or
nore games-within-the-game strikes many players as
ne of Ping-Pong's most appealing features.

Notice, as well, that Ping-Pong employs a logbook
ather than a scorecard. In the first few entries, I have
nserted pings and pongs where they would likely
ccur. From Day 23 onward, I leave the sound effects
o your own imagination and note only the major
actical moves.

Day 1: Digging in his garden one Saturday, Charlie
uffers a sudden attack of back pain. Unable to work,
he watches TV and goes to bed early. The Ping-Pong
Game is about to begin.

Day 2: Charlie can hardly get out of bed. His back is
killing him. He calls his family doctor but learns he is
away for the weekend. The answering service refers
him (ping) to Dr. White. With a supple forehand
stroke, White scribbles a prescription. The pills,
intended to work as pain-killers, only make Charlie
sick at his stomach.

Day 3: Charlie sees his family physician, Dr. Brown.
With a nonchalant backhand return, Brown writes a
different prescription (pong); same medicine, different name, but these pills don't make Charlie sick.

Day 18: Even with sporadic relief provided by the

pills, the pain drives Charlie back to Dr. Brown (ping). Brown deftly lobs him over to a physiotherapis (pong).

Day 23: The physiotherapist, Ms. Green, applies a ho pack and performs a massage.

Days 23 to 37: In these two weeks, Charlie ricochets six times between his home and Ms. Green's office The treatments feel good at the time but after he has driven the two miles to his home, the car seat has made his back as painful as ever.

Day 38: Admitting failure with the hot packs and the massage (net serve), Ms. Green persuades Charlie to try ultrasound (defensive rally) to project heat pain lessly into his spine.

Days 38 to 52: After each of his four trips in for ultrasound his drive home is still murder on Charlie's back.

Day 55: Charlie returns to Dr. Brown's office (change of serve). Disturbed by Charlie's persistent pain, Brown bats him down the hall to X-Ray.

Day 56: Brown is puzzled: Charlie's X-rays are normal, yet his back still hurts. How can that be? He calls Charlie in (feint), recommends further examination (quick save), and flicks him over to an orthopedic surgeon.

Day 121: It's seventeen weeks since the game began. Having waited two months to see the orthopedic surgeon, Dr. Gray, Charlie receives a quick examina tion and a quicker verdict. Here, Gray deftly initiates five other games within the game, beginning with a learned pronouncement: "You have unilateral spon dylolysis." (Speaking Doctor) "I'm afraid there's noth ing I can do for you." (Bogeyman) Ignoring Charlie's questions (Mum's the Word), Gray forehands him a three-page list of don'ts (Thou Shalt Not), and de scribes what will happen if he disregards them (Crys tal Ball). (Gray does not play Double Diagnosis only because Charlie's condition has remained undiag

osed until now.) "You'll just have to live with your
ain," Gray tells Charlie. He suggests checking back
ith Dr. Brown in a couple of weeks.

ay 133: It's Dr. Brown's serve again, but he can't
nink of a new strategy. Forgetting momentarily what
eatments Charlie has had, he suggests pills, hot
acks, massage, ultrasound. . . . For the first time,
harlie distinctly hears the sound of the game in
rogress: ping-pong, ping-pong. He flares up but stops
hort. They're keeping something from him! He visual-
zes himself in a wheelchair. Bewildered and angry, he
torms out of Dr. Brown's office.

ay 134: Charlie calls Dr. Brown, apologizes, and asks
or more pills. He didn't sleep a wink all night. Brown
ently suggests that the problem may be nerves.
Insure by now of his own mental stability, Charlie
asn't the stamina to argue when Brown refers him to
psychiatrist (forehand smash).

Days 168 to 318: In five months of weekly sessions
vith Dr. Black, Charlie probes his psyche back to early
hildhood. From this insight, Black makes a signifi-
ant pronouncement: "There's nothing wrong with
our head. You have back trouble. What you need is an
rthopedic surgeon or at least a careful examination
y your family doctor. When you get your back fixed
p, you may want some psychotherapy. Come and see
ne then."

From here on, Charlie hears without heeding as the
;ame's final rallies become a blur.

Day 332: Gray sees Charlie again and declares him
inchanged: "As I said before, there's nothing I can
lo. . . ." (ping)

Day 339: Brown has heard of a new drug in Minnesota:
Unfortunately, the side effects . . ." (pong)

Day 353: Gray, just back from an international medi-
al symposium, is high on a new surgical technique:
. . . no guarantee, of course, but what else can we do?
And what have you got to lose?" (ping)

Day 364: Brown recalls a spa in Arizona: ". . . prett
expensive, of course, but I've known patients who. .
(pong)

Day 366: On the first anniversary of his back attac
Charlie riffles through the Yellow Pages and finds th
listing he's looking for — Chiropractors. Then anothe
thought strikes him: Frank, down at the office, wa
telling about this acupuncturist who . . .

Charlie's first Ping-Pong game is over. But he wi
soon get another one started — on his own.

The tragedy is that the treatment Charlie needs i
simple, inexpensive, and undramatic. Given the righ
information, even yet, he could become his own mos
effective back doctor. All that's wrong with his back i
a bit of wear and tear from forty-seven years of livin
The pain is real and the psychiatrist is right: there i
nothing wrong with Charlie's head unless you coun
the anxiety that arises from back pain — and from
Ping-Pong.

The treatments Charlie got — the pills, the ho
packs, the massage, the ultrasound — were not neces
sarily useless, but they provided short-term relief a
best. As for the long-term measures — the new
surgical technique, the spa, the chiropractic, th
acupuncture, even the wonder drug — any or all o
them might have proved helpful, but Charlie coul
have done without them if he'd been told, back on Da
3, what he really needed.

He needed a clear idea of what was wrong with hi
back — plus the assurance that his condition wasn'
unusual or serious.

He needed a few days of bed rest — probably a wee
at the most.

He needed to learn a few simple, painless exercise
that can be completed in a few minutes each day.

He needed a new set of daily habits — ways o
sitting, standing, lifting, sleeping — to minimize th
strain on his back.

He needed to realize that you never cure a bad back — you control it.

It sounds far too simple and undramatic to be true. But it is true, as thousands of people have discovered for themselves.

Well, I can hear you saying, there has to be a catch to this somewhere. And you're right — there is a catch. While those simple steps could do wonders for Charlie and for most other people with back trouble, they're impossible to follow unless you understand what your back trouble is all about.

Now that we've dispelled the commonest myths and seen through Bogeyman and Ping-Pong and those other diversions that can sidetrack your efforts to find effective treatment, you're all set to start learning the things you need to know.

3 A Painless Course in Anatomy

I have already rejected the idea that your back is a mysterious and baffling part of your body. We know a great deal about the spine, and the more we learn, the more we appreciate what a truly marvelous piece of machinery it is.

That point was made in an amusing film script I was once asked to check for medical accuracy. The film was to be a short documentary, based on a fanciful premise: a team of engineers is called upon to design a human back without ever having seen one. All that the engineers know at the outset is that some sort of scaffold is needed to support the human body. What could be simpler? They create a solid vertical model resembling a flagpole.

"Sorry," says the client, "but that won't do. Your spine has to be a lot more flexible than that."

The engineers scrap the pole design and fashion a stack of block-like bones. The bones articulate nicely but are forever slipping out of place. The designers hit on the idea of lashing them together with ligaments, the way Indians used to lash thongs around the poles of their wigwams.

"Wait a minute," says the client. "I forgot to tell you — the spine has to bend and rotate — like a construction crane." The engineers spend weeks adding pulleys and guy wires and designing an intricate system of interlocking joints. Several innovations are necessary, including a built-in lubrication system to prevent binding and squeaking, and a series of catches to prevent self-destruction through excessive rotation.

Each time they think they've created the perfect design, some new specification is added. The device has to bear considerable weight, not just at the top but down the sides, too. Their first answer to that challenge, a huge and ugly counterweight, is rejected out of hand. They add extra ligaments and muscles instead. The device has to withstand frequent jostling and bouncing up and down. They design discs as shock-absorbers between the bones. It has to contain a built-in intercom system. They bore a hole down the center and install nerves.

Their creation must have a lifting capacity of 300 pounds per square inch, yet the whole body, spine and all, should weigh no more than 150 pounds, on the average, with some models at less than 100 pounds. Quietly, they scrap their four-ton prototype without even unveiling it.

When they're told to make the whole thing mobile, they mount it on casters, but it keeps skidding about and tipping over. They haven't even solved that problem when the client begins talking wistfully of having "at least one model that can run a four-minute mile." At that point, they throw up their hands and resign en masse. Clearly, no device on earth could possibly meet all those specifications.

Once you consider the demands we place on our spines in the normal course of ordinary living, you no longer wonder why so many people have trouble with their backs. You wonder instead why everybody in the world doesn't suffer back pain.

Patients are always asking, "Why me? Why do I have to be the one with back trouble? Why can't I be normal?"

And I always tell them: "You are normal. It's normal to have back problems. The abnormal people are the ones who don't have back pain."

I always hasten to add that this is no reason to put up with a bad back. But the first point is true: anyone who lives an average lifespan without suffering from backache belongs to a privileged minority. By projecting the statistics on back problems, I have calculated that on any given day, about eleven million people in the United States and Canada are suffering from backache.

Why are so many people susceptible? The answer begins to emerge when you see how your spine is put together, what strains are imposed on it, and what changes it undergoes as your body ages. Marvelous though it is, your spine has its potential weak spots, and if you want to protect them from abuse and prevent them from causing you pain, it's important to know where those weaknesses are and how they develop.

As we all know, your spine consists basically of bones called vertebrae, which are separated and cushioned by oval pads called discs. From the base of your skull through to the bottom of your tailbone, you have thirty-three or thirty-four vertebrae contained in five sections or regions. The three upper regions, which form the mobile part of your spine, have twenty-four vertebrae among them. The two lower regions have nine or ten bones in two fused sections. You have seven vertebrae in your neck or cervical region; twelve in the mid-back, known as the thoracic or dorsal region (these are the vertebrae attached to your ribs); and five vertebrae, the largest of the lot, in the low back or lumbar region. The two immobile sections are the sacrum and the coccyx. (The latter term, pronounced "cock-six," is Latin for cuckoo; the coccyx resembles a cuckoo's bill.) During the formative months before birth, your sacrum was five individual bones, but by the time you were born it had fused into a single bone. Since the sacrum forms the back of your pelvis, it does not require the flexibility of the spinal regions above it. Finally, you have four or

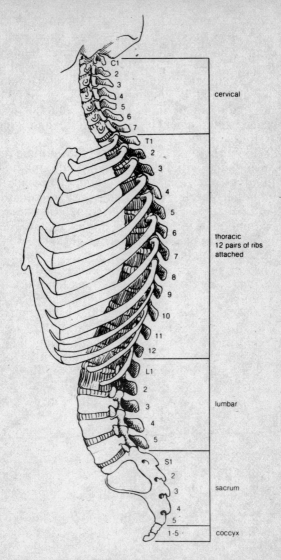

Fig. 1. A side view of the full spine and the five named regions. The cervical and lumbar regions are the most flexible and are the sites of most back pain.

five bones in your tailbone or coccyx. Many people are intrigued to learn that some of us have four coccyx bones while others have five. The coccyx is all that's left of the tail we inherited from the apes a few million years ago, and if you happen to have five coccyx bones, you can perhaps consider yourself a closer relation to our ancient forebears than people who have only four.

I seldom rhyme off the names of those spinal regions to an audience without telling a favorite story of mine. It involves a new medical secretary who had a little trouble deciphering her notes from a dictated letter, specifically a passage that was supposed to read, "He was found to be injured in the lumbar region." Relying on what she remembered hearing, she wrote: "He was shot in the woods."

Throughout this book we'll be concentrating on your spine's cervical and lumbar regions, with occasional mentions of the thoracic, which gives far less trouble than the other two. There wouldn't be any particular reason for you to take note of terms like cervical, thoracic, and lumbar except for one thing: they form the basis of the system doctors use in identifying your vertebrae and the discs that lie between them. If you want to know what your doctor is talking about when he refers to a T_{12} vertebra or an L_2-L_3 disc, take a moment now to learn this system.

It's really quite simple. Your seven cervical (neck) vertebrae are designated from the top down, as C_1, C_2, etc., to C_7. Right below your C_7 is your first thoracic vertebra, T_1. As you'd expect, the rest of the thoracic vertebrae are numbered downward to T_{12}, and then the lumbars take over: L_1 to L_5.

Each disc derives its designation from the vertebrae above and below it. Hence the disc lying between your third and fourth lumbar vertebrae is called your L_3-L_4 disc. This designation is often abbreviated further as simply L_{3-4}. Similarly, the disc between your lowest

thoracic vertebra and your uppermost lumbar vertebra is called the T_{12}-L_1 disc. The lowest disc in your
spine is the L_5-S_1 — that is, the disc between the lowest
of the five lumbar vertebrae and the first of the fused
sacral segments. Although the sacrum shows signs of
having originated as five separate bones, it contains
no discs.

That's all there is to it. And if you feel that your
doctor is "Speaking Doctor" unnecessarily when he
uses these designations, remember that though it may
sound technical and mysterious, it's the only brief and
accurate way of identifying your spinal bones, discs,
and nerves. Otherwise, instead of saying, "Your pain
originates at your L_4 level," your doctor would have to
say, "at the twenty-third vertebra from the top," or
"the fourth vertebra of your lumbar region."

Now let's take a look at your spine and identify the
potential trouble spots.

Each vertebra looks like a squat little drum with an
upright tube fastened to its back. The drum sits with
its flat surfaces at the top and bottom. Extending from
the walls of the tube are several odd-looking projections. Three of these projections are spike-shaped
bones — two extending sideways like wings, and the
third, with a knobby end on it, pointing straight back.
This third spike, and others like it on other vertebrae,
are the knobby bones that can be felt when you run
your fingers up and down your back or somebody
else's. This is the only part of the backbone you can
feel from outside your body. And while those knobby
ends may feel as though they are just under the skin,
they are actually well below the surface — about half
an inch below in a thin person and as much as two
inches below in an overweight one. Which means it's a
long way in from the surface of the skin to the center of
the drum-shaped part of your vertebra — perhaps
three inches in a person of normal weight and maybe
five or six inches in a heavy person. That's a critical

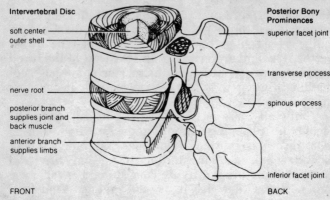

Intervertebral Disc

soft center
outer shell

nerve root

posterior branch
supplies joint and
back muscle

anterior branch
supplies limbs

Posterior Bony
Prominences

superior facet joint

transverse process

spinous process

inferior facet joint

FRONT   BACK

Fig. 2. A spinal unit consists of any two vertebrae and the
intervening disc. The nerve root between the two bones
sends branches to the facet joint and the spinal muscle. Here
the upper disc has been cut to show its central nucleus.

point to keep in mind whenever someone talks as
though the spine were something just under your skin
that he could grab hold of and move around.

Each vertebra has two other pairs of bony parts
jutting towards the back of your body. One pair
extends from the top corners of the tube, the other pair
from the bottom corners. The lower projections extend
downward to interlock with the upper projections of
the vertebra below. Where these projections make
contact they form the joints called facet joints. In that
manner every vertebra is interlocked with its neigh-
bors, in two long, parallel ridges of interlocking joints
on either side of the ridge of your backbone. Between
these interlocking joints, the outer wall of each vertebral tube — that is, the part of the wall closest to the
skin of your back — overlaps its neighbor below, like
the overlapping scales of a fish. These overlapping
walls (called laminae), along with the interlocking
joints and the bony projections described earlier, form
a shield of bone that protects the contents of the spinal
canal.

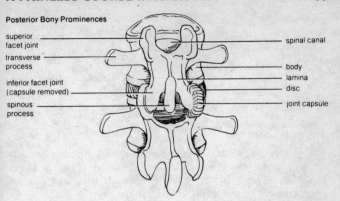

Posterior Bony Prominences

superior facet joint

transverse process

inferior facet joint (capsule removed)

spinous process

spinal canal

body

lamina

disc

joint capsule

Fig. 3. Seen from behind, the spine presents a bony shield which protects the contents of the spinal canal. The tough capsule enclosing each facet joint adds extra stability. The bony projections to each side are for muscle attachment.

The projections that form the facet joints are capped with cartilage — the same kind of smooth, white cartilage you have seen on the knobby end of a chicken leg. The purpose of the cartilage, of course, is to permit ready movement of the joints, which are about the size of the joints in your fingers. Each joint is tightly encased in a strong, fibrous capsule that prevents the joint from coming apart. The joint is so secure inside its capsule that it is actually easier to dislocate your shoulder than it is to dislocate a facet joint.

All in all, it's a highly effective joint system. If the smooth surfaces of the joints become roughened through wear, however, or if a joint tightens up under pressure, the bones grind against each other, and you've got joint pain.

Between the drum-shaped sections of the vertebrae lie the discs. Each disc is tightly bonded, top and bottom, to the adjacent vertebrae above and below — so tightly that it cannot possibly slip out of place the way some people imagine. This bonding effect is so strong, in fact, that if you suffered an extreme blow to

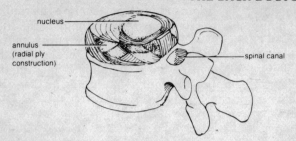

Fig. 4. The disc's outer layers have a radial ply construction to add strength. Its jelly-filled center acts as a shock absorber. The top and bottom of each disc are bonded permanently to the adjacent vertebrae.

your spine — say, in an automobile accident — the vertebral bones would likely give way before any of the discs would budge. By separating and cushioning the vertebrae from each other, the disc helps support the weight of your head and upper body and absorbs the shock of any unusual load or sudden downward pressure.

If you could examine a disc from somebody's spine, you would find that it has a tough, elastic shell made of criss-crossed layers of fibers like the plies in a radial belted tire. In fact, you might even wonder whether the designers of modern automobile tires got the idea from studying spinal discs. If you looked inside the disc you would find a soft substance about the consistency of jelly. And, like the jelly desserts you make from powders, this material is mostly water. Since it's the water that gives the disc its cushiony character, much like the water in a waterbed, you can imagine what happens if the disc dries up.

Let's take a closer look now at the tube-like structure on the back of the drum — the part known as the spinal canal, which encases your spinal cord. Most people think of the canal as a cylinder-like pipeline. In reality, it is a five-sided tunnel resembling the outline of one of those little houses used in playing the game of

Monopoly. The sloping sides that look like the roof of the house are the laminae, which help form that protective shield we described earlier. Figure 5 shows this shape clearly. Notice how closely the "floor" of the house is positioned to the drum-shaped part of the vertebra and to the adjacent disc. As long as that disc retains its shape, the system functions well; if it doesn't, you're looking at another trouble spot.

As you might expect, your back muscles also play a part in any back trouble you may have. But, contrary to what you may have always assumed, your spine does not have one long, thin muscle running from top to tailbone. Most of your back muscles are fairly small, working in pairs or threesomes, each spanning only two or three vertebrae. The only really large muscle in your back is the one that weight-lifters work so hard to develop. It's called the trapezius, and it's a kite-shaped structure, with one point at the tip of your skull, two opposite points at the outer edges of your shoulders, and the fourth point halfway down the center of your back.

Your back muscles can be associated with back pain in three ways, all of them involving spasm, a tensing-up process commonly referred to as cramps. The muscular spasms that occur in your back are essentially the same as those familiar, painful cramps we all get at times in the calves of our legs through to the arches of our feet. In your back, a spasm may occur as a muscular reaction to painful wear and tear, in a facet joint for instance. Or, even without physical cause, a back muscle may go into spasm in response to emotional stress. Or, a muscle already in spasm may cause other muscles to go into spasm, thereby radiating tension and pain to other parts of your spine.

And of course there is a close relationship between back pain and the nerves in and around your spine. In some instances, a nerve itself may be the actual site of your trouble, if it is being irritated by pressure from some other part of the spine, such as a disc. In other

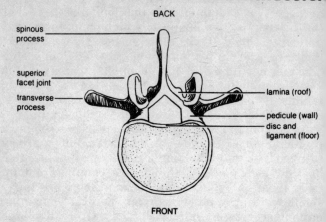

BACK

spinous
process

superior
facet joint

transverse
process

lamina (roof)

pedicule (wall)

disc and
ligament (floor)

FRONT

Fig. 5. The five-sided shape of the spinal canal resembles
a Monopoly house. The floor of the canal is alternately bone
on the back of the vertebra and a strong ligament covering
the intervertebral disc. Two facet joints and three bony
prominences project from the roof; these are for muscle
attachment.

instances, a nerve, or several nerves, may simply be
serving as the "telephone lines" communicating the
message from the nerve ends to the brain, signaling
that such-and-such a body part is being pressed,
squeezed, rubbed, or otherwise irritated. So let's take
a look at your nervous system and see in more detail
how it relates to your back problems.

If you've ever peeked inside an old-style television
set and seen the confusing array of wire "spaghetti"
that predated printed circuitry, you can begin to
imagine the great complexity of nerves centered in
your spinal canal.

All along your spinal column there are small openings between the bony projections of adjacent vertebrae. These openings serve as passages for pairs of
nerves branching out, right and left, from the spinal

BACK

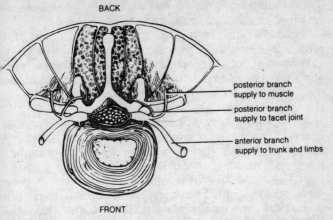

posterior branch
supply to muscle

posterior branch
supply to facet joint

anterior branch
supply to trunk and limbs

FRONT

Fig. 6. Branches of the spinal nerve roots serve the back muscle, facet joints, and outer layers of the disc. As it leaves the spinal canal, each nerve root must pass directly over the back corner of the disc.

cord. These main branches, or nerve roots as they are often called, split off into lesser branches, some to serve the spine itself, others the limbs and the rest of the body.

The nerves of your spine are divided into the same sections as the vertebrae and are given the same designations — C_1, T_1, L_1, and so on — but with one minor variation. Because there are eight cervical nerves, compared to only seven cervical vertebrae, the C series for nerves runs to C_8, while the C series for vertebrae stops at C_7.

Nerve roots from the lower cervical area come together to form major branches that pass below your shoulders and into your arms. For this reason, if you have trouble in your neck, you may feel pain in your shoulder. Similarly, nerve roots from the lower lumbar and upper sacral areas join together to form the sciatic nerve, which runs down the back of your leg.

This explains why you sometimes suffer leg pains as a result of trouble in your lower back.

Since every nerve root leaves the spinal canal at a point close to a disc, passing through a narrow bony exit formed by the vertebrae above and below, and since the size of that exit depends on the height of the disc, you can see how a nerve might get into trouble if the disc becomes flatter than normal.

Apart from its service to the rest of your body, your central nervous system is connected to virtually every part of your back through a network of small branches from each nerve root. These connections are made to your vertebrae and facet joints, the outer part of your discs (though not the centers), the muscles that give your back movement and flexibility, and the ligaments that tie the whole structure together.

Although most people think of the spinal cord as merely a conduit between the brain and the body, it in fact carries out certain functions that were once credited exclusively to the brain. When your doctor gives you that familiar reflex test by tapping your knee lightly with a rubber mallet, the impulses race up your leg as far as the spinal cord — but no farther. Your spinal cord responds to the impulses by "ordering" a muscular reaction.

In response to back pain, your spinal cord performs an intermediate function, processing raw information received from the nerve ends and relaying this information, in more refined form, to the brain.

It's a system that could be compared to the creation of a simple photograph. At the scene of the picture-taking, light enters the lens to record an image on the film. Carried into the darkroom, the film is processed by a technician who neither knows nor cares what it depicts. Finally the picture is passed along to the photographer, who is the first to identify the likeness of lovable old Aunt Tilly squinting at us from her front porch. With back pain, the sequence is: impulses at the nerve ends, processing in the spinal cord — in the dark, so to speak — and identification of the message by the brain as pain.

Every communications system has its limitations, and in this one, the spinal cord can't tell which of the mini-branches and secondary branches carried that message into the main nerve branch. This is one reason why a doctor may find it difficult to localize a back problem from what you can say about where you feel your pain. You may have to admit, "I don't know whether the pain is coming from my knee or the back of my thigh, or my buttock or the low part of my back." When that happens, you are experiencing the phenomenon doctors call referred pain.

There are other reasons why you may be misled about the actual source of your pain. For instance, that big trapezius muscle on your upper back may pick up pain sensations from your lower back and transmit them to the back of your neck. Or your back muscles may create additional pain in a secondary area by reacting to irritation felt by, say, a facet joint. While the joint irritation is translated into pain by the spinal cord, the muscle at the scene of the trouble may respond by tightening up. This is a protective reaction intended to immobilize the irritated area and thus prevent further irritation. Ironically, however, this reaction may be so severe that it produces pain of its own. You may not recognize this condition for what it is — a muscle spasm or cramp; you may think your whole back has "gone out." And unless you know more than most people know about back problems, you probably wouldn't believe me if I told you that the culprit in this whole affair is just one tiny but irritable spinal joint no bigger than the joint in one of your thumbs.

Here's how a little case of facet-joint pain in the lumbar area can become magnified:

1. The pain, caused by normal wear and tear, originates in a small joint.

2. The initial impulse is transmitted into the main

nerve and along to the spinal cord, where it is processed as back pain.

3. The impulse courses throughout the length of the nerve, which, as it happens, also runs down into the leg. Now you have leg pain as well as back pain.

4. The muscles in the affected area react by going into spasm. Now you have muscular pain as well as leg pain and back pain.

5. Because the action is taking place on one side of your body, your spine is forced to curve unnaturally to that side as the muscles contract.

6. Other muscles respond by tightening up in new spasms. You are now virtually immobile.

In short, one little trouble spot in the facet joint becomes responsible for creating back pain, leg pain, muscular pain in various locations, and loss of movement of one side, possibly both sides, of your body. No wonder your doctor may have trouble diagnosing your problem, and no wonder you're convinced that you have something far more serious than simple irritation of a spinal joint. And isn't it easy to see why so many people are frightened unnecessarily by a condition that can be traced to a source of trouble which is not permanent and which, in itself, is not even serious?

You may be wondering whether the things I've been saying about low-back pain apply as well to neck pain. In general, the answer is yes. There are differences, however, that have to do with mobility and your awareness of what's going on in that portion of your spine.

Your neck, being designed for greater mobility than the lower parts of your spine, is obviously more susceptible to any troubles arising from movement of the joints. And since the cervical or neck region of your spine is closer to the surface and encased in less fat and muscle, you are always more aware of anything that is going on there. For instance, your neck may readily emit the cracking sounds that occur normally with extensive movement of your spinal joints, and

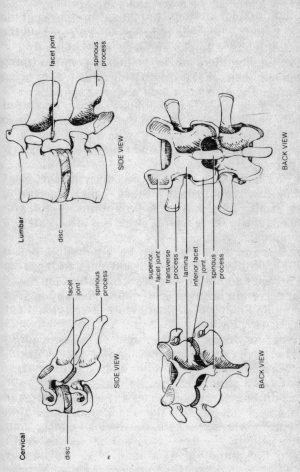

Fig. 7. A comparison of side and back views of the cervical and lumbar spine. The larger, lumbar vertebrae are designed to carry weight, while the smaller, mobile vertebrae permit free movement of the head. Facet joints in the cervical region are more flexible but less stable than those in the low back.

Lumbar

facet joint

spinous process

SIDE VIEW

disc

BACK VIEW

Cervical

facet joint

spinous process

SIDE VIEW

disc

superior facet joint

transverse process

lamina

inferior facet joint

spinous process

BACK VIEW

you will hear those sounds more easily because the joints are near the surface and close to your ears.

Neck pain can be as deceiving about its origins as lower-back pain. Just as pain in your low back radiates into your buttocks and legs, neck pain radiates into your shoulders and arms. Just as people with back pain may believe it is originating in their hips or buttocks, people with neck pain are often convinced that the problem is in their shoulders.

I usually check for this radiation effect by conducting a simple test with anyone who complains of shoulder pain: take your hand and cover the part that is most painful. If you cover the top of your shoulder, I suspect you have neck pain. If you cover the side of your shoulder, you probably have pain from the shoulder itself. This test is not infallible, but it's accurate enough to serve well as an early and easy step in my diagnosis.

As we'll see in a later chapter, neck pain does not respond as readily as low-back pain does to therapeutic exercises and improved postural habits. On the other hand, certain forms of professional therapy such as traction and manipulation are more effective with necks than with backs.

Finally, a few words about the biomechanics of your spine. The load exerted on the discs of your spine changes dramatically from one body position to another. Even a slight shift in position can make an enormous difference. For instance, if you are sitting at a desk in an upright position the load is moderate, but if you bend forward, you increase the load considerably. Surprisingly, the stress on the disc is less severe when you are standing erect than when you are slumped forward at a desk. But, regardless of your position, if that load happens to be exerted on a worn disc, you'll feel pain. The relative loads imposed during various postures were documented in a Swedish study involving the insertion of needles into the discs of living subjects. The results, shown in Figure 8,

Fig. 8. This diagram illustrates the relative pressures within the third lumbar disc in various positions. Pressure is least while lying on the back and greatest while sitting forward. Interdiscal pressure is generally higher when sitting than when standing. (After Nachemson)

make it clear that if you have a disc affected by wear and tear, the position of your back during routine tasks is crucial.

Early in this chapter, I made the point that we all impose incredible demands on our backs, just in the course of everyday living. Imagine a ten-pound package sitting on a table. You reach out to lift it at arm's length. In holding your arm out, away from your body, you automatically use muscles in your back. Your lifting action becomes comparable to the action of a children's seesaw. If the package is to be raised, there must be enough downward thrust in your spinal area to offset the weight of the package and provide lift.

Ordinarily, a seesaw has the same amount of plank on each side of the fulcrum or center point. Now, if you move the fulcrum so that there is, say, three times as much plank on one side as on the other, the person on the short end has to exert three times as much downward pressure (or add that much extra weight) just to maintain equilibrium. In other words, he's working against a ratio of three to one.

The same principle applies when you raise a package at arm's length, but the ratio is far greater. If your total reach from mid-spine to finger grasp is twenty-five inches, and the distance from mid-spine to your back muscles is one inch, you're working against a twenty-five-to-one ratio. That means you must provide 250 pounds plus of downward thrust just to lift that ten-pound package. Chances are that your back muscles won't supply that much force — certainly not without considerable strain. To spread the load, you bring your belly muscles into play.

How do they help? Let's go back to the seesaw for a moment. This time we move the fulcrum to provide a twenty-five-to-one ratio — so that we are accurately representing the lift problem you have with the package. But now we support the long arm of the seesaw by slipping a giant coil spring under it just a short distance from the fulcrum. The coil spring

Fig. 9. With the same length on each side, the seesaw is balanced by two people of the same weight. As the lengths change, the balance is lost. Additional support from the spring helps solve the problem without increasing the load on the short side.

provides much of the lift, and so it's no longer necessary for the person on the short end to exert the entire 250-pound downward pressure.

Your belly muscles can perform much the same function as that coil spring. By tightening those muscles during the lift, you redistribute some of the exertion, so that the load is shared by your back muscles and your belly muscles, without excessive strain on either. Which leads me to a point I will be stressing in later chapters on exercise, sports, and good posture: strong belly muscles are essential in maintaining a pain-free back. For, apart from their value in helping your back maintain its best posture, they share loads that could otherwise create back strain. Competitive weight-lifters have been exploiting that principle for years. Isn't it time you began to exploit it for the benefit of your own back?

Now that you have an elementary understanding of how your spine is designed and how it functions, you're ready to appreciate what happens to it when some of its parts are thrown out of kilter by wear and tear or the process of aging. But before we begin our rundown on the causes of back pain, let's devote a chapter to the commonest types — and see which of them comes closest to describing your condition.

4 Are You Type One, Type Two, or Type Three?

Suppose that you and I had never met until you walked up to me at a social gathering and said, "Hello, I'm So-and-so. I understand you're a back specialist. I have this pain right here in my lower back. What do you think is wrong?"

Now, in the best medical tradition — and to cut down on my malpractice costs — I'd feel obliged to reply, "I'm sorry, but I wouldn't hazard a guess without first discussing your medical history and symptoms and examining you in my office."

Secretly I'd be tempted to say, "I'll bet you nine to one that you've got either a worn facet joint or a protruding disc."

How could I be so sure? Well, I wouldn't really know. But my informed guess would be a pretty safe bet. First, I would assume that you hadn't injured your back in an accident; if you had, you wouldn't be asking me what was wrong — you'd already know. Second, I'd assume that your back problem was not part of a generalized disease. If it were, you might have other symptoms and you wouldn't likely describe your condition simply as back pain.

By deduction, then, I would conclude that you probably have one of the three most common types of back problems: a worn facet joint, which I call Type One backache; a protruding disc, Type Two; or a pinched nerve, Type Three. And since Type Three accounts for only about one case of common backache out of every ten, there is a ninety-percent chance that you have Type One or Type Two.

So you can see that while my silent and instant diagnosis of your trouble wasn't foolproof — deduction seldom is — statistically I had a very good chance of being right. An experienced doctor makes judgments of this sort every day. He begins a diagnosis with the broad assumption that a patient's condition is as commonplace as the obvious symptoms suggest. As he proceeds with the diagnosis, he protects himself and his patient from the danger of error by including observations and tests that will either rule out or point to some less common condition. And of course if there is evidence of an unusual problem, he'll take special steps to check it out. Since his days in medical school, however, he has had it drummed into his head that "Common things happen most commonly." And he has probably heard the same principle enunciated in the expression, "When you hear hoofbeats, think horses, not zebras."

Most of us follow that principle in the course of everyday living, whether we realize it or not. Suppose, for instance, that you have a house guest who is about to borrow your car. He walks out with your keys and two minutes later he comes back to say that the car won't start. Immediately, you assume there's just some minor problem: maybe the car is out of gas, or the battery is low, or the carburetor is acting up. You don't jump to the conclusion that the engine block is cracked or that the pistons have suddenly seized up. These things happen to automobiles, but you don't assume at the outset that your car has serious trouble.

We all apply that sort of common sense when we have trouble with our cars. But, for some reason, when people have trouble with their backs, common sense flies out the window. Instead of assuming that their trouble is ordinary, minor, and temporary, people allow the pain to convince them that they must have some dread disease.

If you have been harboring that sort of fear about your back condition, I urge you to reconsider: in the absence of any evidence to the contrary, try assuming for the time being that you have one of the common forms of back trouble. For what I am proposing to do here is to help you discover, by yourself, whether your problem is Type One, Type Two, or Type Three.

You will have plenty of opportunity later to let your doctor explore the rarer possibilities, if he sees any reason to do so. In any case, there's no risk involved in checking your condition against the descriptions I give you here; in fact, the exercise will help prepare you to answer your own doctor's questions more accurately and precisely, thereby saving time and avoiding any misunderstanding that could hamper diagnosis and delay treatment.

It should almost go without saying that I don't expect you to conduct a self-examination while you are in severe pain. If you are immobilized with muscle spasms or emotionally upset by your pain, put this book aside and come back to it after you've rested enough to be on the road to temporary recovery. My questions and tests are intended for use while your pain is present but more or less tolerable, or while you are waiting patiently for your next acute attack.

Let's begin by making sure that your pain is originating in your back, not in your hip — which is one of the sites most often confused with back pain. Try these two tests.

Lying on your back, draw your knees up to your chest. If that causes pain in your groin, you may have hip trouble.

Now, with the knees still bent, turn your lower legs out. If that gentle twisting motion hurts, you may have hip trouble. In that case, movement will again cause pain in your groin and perhaps down the front of your thigh to the knee.

No problem so far? Then let's move on to rule out trauma as the cause of your back pain. If you can't remember being injured, your back problem is not a case of accidental damage. Any accident serious

enough to cause severe pain weeks or months later
would be a major and memorable incident: perhaps an
auto collision, a painful fall, or a serious incident such
as the war injury that caused John F. Kennedy back
pain for years.

With trauma eliminated, what about disease? You
can rule that out, too, if you can answer yes to all three
of these questions:

1. Does your back feel better after a good rest?
2. Does each acute attack of pain pretty well disappear in about two weeks? (Recognizing that
   another attack could occur soon after the first
   one.)
3. Are you free of accompanying symptoms such as
   fever; weight loss; skin rashes; problems with
   other joints, particularly in your fingers, toes,
   hips, and knees; or persistent morning stiffness
   in your back even after the pain is gone?

Even if you answered no to one or more of those
questions, your problem is not necessarily a disease.
The odds remain strong in favor of common backache.

If you have passed the test so far, you can be
reasonably certain that you have Type One, Type
Two, or Type Three back pain, or, at the most, some
combination of them. All three types, incidentally, are
what our forefathers used to call lumbago, which is an
archaic term meaning low-back pain.

To help determine whether you have Type One,
Type Two, or Type Three backache, study the descriptions that follow. Be sure to read all three descriptions,
because their symptoms and characteristics overlap
to some extent. In fact, during the acute phase it may
be impossible to distinguish the pain of one type from
that of another. Also, take note that while these
descriptions are typical, they cannot apply to everyone's case of common back pain. Unusual variations
may develop to create symptoms that are not typical.
Besides, some people have more than one type of
condition, and others experience varying symptoms

over a period of time because they are afflicted by two or three types in succession.

See which of these descriptions comes closest to defining your form of back pain.

Type One: The Worn Facet

Your trouble begins with a minor incident of routine exertion, such as picking up a garden hoe or retrieving a golf ball. The attack of back pain may be almost immediate, or its intensity may increase rapidly for a day or two after the incident. The pain is accentuated when you arch your back, as you would when you lean back to look up at the ceiling. Bending forward helps ease the pain, and so you tend to stand and walk that way. Straightening up is painful.

Your pain is mainly in your low back. It may radiate into your buttocks and down the back part of one or both legs as far as the knee. There is no pain, however, in your lower legs or feet. Usually, one leg is more painful than the other.

If you were asked to place your hands on the most painful area, you would probably reach back to indicate the top of your buttocks. If you exert a little pressure there, you can easily feel two bony lumps located at the top of your pelvis. These lumps are normal, of course; they are at the upper points of your sacroiliac joints. These are not the points where your pain is originating, but your muscle spasm makes it feel as though they were. Sacroiliac joints used to be blamed for a great deal of back pain a few years ago, before doctors learned everything they now know about facet pain.

With rest, or at least in the absence of any aggravation, your acute pain disappears within four to fourteen days. This pattern of recovery is welcome, but it can also be embarrassing. Many a Type One patient has been in great agony while arranging a doctor's

appointment, only to find the pain gone on the day of
the appointment. Don't be embarrassed if this happens
to you. Keep your appointment anyway and report the
sequence of events. A good back doctor won't be
surprised to hear that your pain has come and gone,
and he will use the information as an important clue in
your diagnosis.

Your attack may never recur. But if it does, its most
typical pattern will be recurrences two or three times a
year.

Type Two: The Protruding Disc

Type Two has many of the same characteristics as
Type One, but it also has these distinguishing differences: a Type Two attack may begin with the same
sort of incident as Type One, but the onset of pain is
likely to be less sharp and immediate; more often it
will build up slowly, over a couple of days, from mild
discomfort to severe pain. The pain will recede notice-
ably in a week or two, but, unlike Type One pain, it
won't disappear. Instead, it will linger on as a nagging
backache, or, in some cases, as an intense and constant
pain.

In contrast with Type One, Type Two isn't aggravated more when you bend back; it's bending forward
that intensifies the pain. Consequently, you prefer to
stand erect and avoid bending forward. Like Type
One, Type Two pain is felt mainly in the back,
although it may radiate into your buttocks and legs,
just as Type One does.

The One-Two Combination

So far, we have dealt with Type One and Type Two
as separate sources of pain, which in fact they are. The
causes of these two types of backache, however, are
closely interrelated, as you will discover in the next
chapter. And because of this close relationship, it is

possible for you to have a combination of Type One and Type Two. To test this possibility, check your history carefully.

Do you find you have acute, short-term attacks interspersed with longer-lasting attacks? Perhaps you have noticed that not all your attacks begin in the same way or last the same amount of time.

Is your pain aggravated when you bend backward *and* forward? If so, you could have two sources of pain — a facet joint (Type One) and a disc (Type Two). Your problem is not necessarily any worse if you have both types in combination, but it may be more difficult to diagnose.

A Negative Test for Types One and Two

Most readers will identify with the symptoms of either Type One or Type Two, since these account for nine out of every ten cases of common back pain. Readers who don't feel that their condition has been described so far may be tempted to skip ahead from here to see whether their symptoms are set out under Type Three. Instead, I suggest that every reader take the simple test I describe next, because it provides a useful clue about all three types of pain.

This test will be negative in cases of Type One or Type Two back pain; that is, it will not cause pain if your problem is only Type One or Type Two. Therefore, it can be used by Type One and Type Two people to confirm that they do not have a Type Three problem — the pinched nerve. Obviously, readers who believe they may be Type Three ought to try this test too.

Before doing so, it is important to understand that a nerve can be subjected to pressure without losing its ability to function. When we talk about Type Three back pain, we are referring to symptoms that merely indicate that a nerve is being irritated; the nerve's function may or may not have been disrupted. If nerve conduction has been impaired, you have a degree of

Type Three pain that is more serious than mere irritation. It is the irritation of a nerve, however, that distinguishes Type Three from the other two types of common back pain. The following test, described in two parts, is designed specifically to determine whether you have an irritated spinal nerve.

A. Lying on your back, try lifting one leg with the knee straight. If you cannot manage the lift alone, have someone help raise the leg gently for you. Does this action produce new pain, as distinct from the existing pain in your back and legs? If you have Type Three trouble, the pain caused by leg-lifting will be felt as far as the back of your knee or even down to your toes. This test may cause back pain, but it is not significant; it's the leg pain, or lack of it, that matters. All that the back pain indicates is the presence of Type One or Type Two trouble in the back itself, which, no doubt, you already recognize.

B. Now take note of the degree to which you can lift that leg, or allow it to be lifted for you. Don't expect to lift it to form a right angle, which is ninety degrees; only people who do this exercise regularly can manage that. But can you manage to lift it more than two-thirds of a right angle, that is, more than sixty degrees, without leg pain? If not, you may have Type Three back trouble.

Type Three: A Pinched Nerve

People think of a pinched nerve as a condition entirely separate from the other two types of backache. Actually, Type Three could just as well be known as Type Two Plus — that is, a protruding disc plus a pinched nerve. For it is a protruding disc, you see, that presses against or "pinches" a pinched nerve. When you know that fact, you won't be surprised to learn that Type Three backache exhibits all the symptoms of Type Two, along with several of its own. As with Type Two,

Type Three backache comes on over a period of a day or two. The pain builds and stays for weeks. And whenever you bend forward, the pain is worse. These are all symptoms of a protruding disc.

Because you also have a pinched or irritated nerve, you have other symptoms which are peculiar to Type Three. You have pain running into your legs, but it doesn't stop at the knees, as leg pain does with the other types. Instead, it reaches the lower leg and, in many cases, spreads into the feet and toes. What's more, your leg pain is even worse than your back pain. Typically, a patient with Type Three pain will say to me, "My problem is not really my back — it's my legs."

When the diagnosis of a pinched nerve is made, the concern must obviously be whether or not the pressure is sufficient to damage the nerve's function. In Type Three back pain, tests of power, reflexes, and sensation are important. Negative results (that is, results indicating that your responses are normal) will support the diagnosis of Type One or Type Two back pain, or Type Three trouble with nerve irritation only. These three groups comprise the great majority of cases, and only rarely will the tests described here show positive findings. If you suspect you have Type Three pain, I recommend you try these tests to confirm the nerve's ability to transmit messages. Patients with Type One or Type Two back pain may wish to try them as well, since negative results strengthen those diagnoses.

As you set out to take these tests, do your best to adopt an objective attitude about your findings. Try hard not to exaggerate the results in your mind. I know it's impossible to be completely objective and dispassionate about the condition of your own body, but do your best to record your findings as if you were reporting on someone else's condition — some friend whose ailment would cause you to feel concerned but not upset or alarmed.

1. Test your muscle power

This is the most accurate and hence the most signifi- cant test you can conduct to determine a loss of nerve function. In Type One or Type Two pain, or with simple nerve irritation in Type Three, you should have normal muscle power. In the circumstances, it may be painful to use that power, but the power should still be there. In other words, don't be misled by the fact that your pain inhibits or restricts your movement; that is to be expected. It is quite another thing to find that your muscles will not deliver normal power during these two tests.

A. Can you raise yourself easily to a tiptoe position, that is, up onto the balls of your feet, and back down again? If you're a person of middle age or younger, you will normally be able to raise and lower your heels and arches this way, ten times on both feet at once, and ten times on each foot separately while standing on one leg.

B. Can you walk on your heels? While standing with your feet comfortably apart, raise your toes and arches as high as you can off the floor and see if you can walk that way — that is, with your weight entirely on your heels. It's an awkward gait at the best of times, but apart from the fact that it may aggravate your present back pain, you should be able to do this as well as you ever could.

If you can pass both muscular tests, it is unlikely that you have a loss of normal nerve activity.

2. Test the reflexes in your knees and ankles

This is the second most significant of the three groups of tests in this series. The significance of this test does not depend on whether your reflexes are strong or weak, but rather on whether they have undergone any distinct change, or whether there is a pronounced difference in the reflexes of one leg compared with the other. You may find it much easier to have someone test your reflexes for you.

If you had strong reflexes in the past, before the onset of your back problems, and if you discover now that your reflexes are weak, this could be a significant finding. Or, if you discover that your reflexes are far stronger in one leg than in the other, you should make a note of this fact and report it to your doctor when you see him. But, as with the muscular tests, it's the negative results that count most: the normal reactions indicating that you do not have Type Three back trouble with a loss of nerve function.

A. Test your knee reflexes first — they're easier. Equip yourself with a small, heavy object that will serve as a hammer. A heavy book, say, three-quarters of an inch thick, will do if you use the book's spine as the hammering surface. Sit on a chair of normal height and cross your legs at the knee so that one leg is dangling. Now use your makeshift hammer to strike the soft area of your knee right below the kneecap. It may take two or three tries, but if you do it right, your leg should kick upward in a sudden, involuntary motion. If that well-known knee-jerk reaction occurs, the reflexes in that knee are normal. Now cross your legs in the opposite way and repeat the test on the other knee. Compare this second reaction with the first. If your knee reflexes have been tested this way in the past, consider whether any change has occurred in your reflex ability. If your responses seem about the same for both legs, and if they seem unchanged from your presumably normal past, it is unlikely that you have nerve damage.

B. Test your ankle reflexes in a similar way. In a sitting position, remove your shoes and place the calf of one leg across the other knee, leaving your ankle and foot projecting out to one side, well clear of the opposite thigh. Now perform the same hammering

action on the back of your foot, right above the heel —
across that cord that most people know as their
Achilles' tendon. If you perform this action correctly
your foot should jerk downwards. Test both of your
ankles this way. If someone is doing this test for you
you should kneel on a chair with your ankles hanging
free while the other person taps gently first on one
tendon and then the other. Once you get reactions on
both ankles, consider whether they are more or less
the same. If they are, again it is unlikely that you have
an impaired nerve.

3. Test your legs for sensory ability

This is the least reliable of the three types of tests in
this series because feelings are subjective. Whereas
muscles and reflex tests produce results that you or
your doctor can observe and evaluate, a sensory test
relies entirely on your subjective judgment of what
you feel.

The idea of this test is to see whether you have
experienced any loss of sensation in certain parts of
your legs. A loss of sensation is not to be confused
with a tingling or "funny feeling" in one or both legs.
What we are looking for here is a true inability to feel
the split second of pain you normally get from a
pinprick in the skin.

To conduct this test, bare your feet and lower legs.
Equip yourself with a safety-pin. Seated in any
position you find comfortable, reach down and, using
a short and rapid jabbing motion, prick yourself in the
three test areas in succession: first, on the inner part of
one foot, just below the big toe; second, on the opposite
side of the foot, just below your little toe; and, third, on
the calf along the inside of your leg. Repeat this test on
the other foot and leg.

If you feel normal pain from each of these locations,
it is unlikely that you have a disruption in the nerve's
ability to conduct impulses. By deduction, then, your

back pain is probably Type One or Type Two, or Type Three with only nerve-root irritation.

If you have conducted these tests carefully and evaluated the results as objectively as possible, you should now have a pretty good idea whether your back trouble is Type One, Type Two, or Type Three. Take note that these designations mean what they say: that is, they are *types* of back conditions, not rankings from "least bad" to "worst."

It may make better cocktail-party conversation to describe yourself as the victim of a pinched nerve, the rarest of the three types. But Type Three is not necessarily worse than either of the other two — it's just different, and may require different treatment. While there is no such thing as a "good" kind of backache, each type has its own advantages — if you can call them that — as well as its drawbacks.

Type One: A worn facet may lack drama, but if this is your problem, look at it this way: at least you have plenty of company — lots of opportunities to swap symptoms and sympathy with your fellow sufferers. And don't underrate the advantage of having a pain that disappears completely between attacks.

Type Two: Your protruding disc obviously makes more appealing social conversation than Type One's worn facet. You may even indulgently allow friends to refer to your "slipped disc," even though you know by now that discs don't slip. And, incidentally, they don't "disintegrate" either, as we'll see in the next chapter. One drawback to being a Type Two is the way the pain lingers on, between attacks, as a dull ache. But keep reading. Help is on the way.

Type Three: As I pointed out in Chapter One, this is the problem most back sufferers think they have — and most of them, of course, are wrong. You Type Threes are an exclusive group. On the other hand, while I would not for a moment make light of your pain, I have to say again that your pinched nerve is not necessarily as painful as it sounds, and it may be less painful than a worn facet or a protruding disc. Just the same, you are more likely to need professional help in bringing your problem under permanent control.

Whatever type you believe you are, or even if you suspect you have two or three types all at once, take comfort from the fact that bed rest will do wonders for acute back pain, and that, thanks to the natural healing process, all bad backs tend to get better by themselves. Perhaps you will appreciate that last point more fully after you have read the next chapter on the causes of common backache.

5 The Causes of Your Back Pain

Now that you have a good idea whether you are a Type One, a Type Two, or a Type Three pain sufferer, you will want to learn more about the specific origins of your condition.

Let's take a detailed look at the causes of common backache, beginning — as your spine itself so often does — with disc trouble. As you recall from Chapter Three, the discs in your spine contain a jelly-like substance that is mostly water. This fluid is being constantly renewed, courtesy of your bloodstream. Using a chemical action, the "jelly" inside the disc absorbs the moisture from small blood vessels nearby. Meanwhile, during the course of a normal day, the weight of your body squeezes some of the moisture out, allowing it to return to the bloodstream. This cycling process results in the loss of a bit of height while you are up and around. You will regain that height each night as you lie sleeping. If you are young and tall and if your discs are healthy, you will routinely lose and regain as much as a half-inch of height every twenty-four hours. You may have noticed that when you set out to drive home from work in the evening, you have to adjust your rear-vision mirror because you are a little shorter than when you drove to work that morning.

A dramatic demonstration of this phenomenon took place in 1974, when three U.S. astronauts returned to earth after eighty-four days aboard Skylab, the orbiting space station. To the amazement of their families and the doctors at NASA, the space travelers were each almost two inches taller than they were when they left on the voyage. During those twelve weeks in orbit, their bloodstreams had continued carrying moisture into the discs of their spines; but with no gravity to enforce the other part of the exchange process, their discs fattened up with moisture, making their spines longer and the men taller. Once they returned to earth, gravity took over again, and within a few days the astronauts were back to normal size. Since that mission, space suits have been designed to accommodate such stretching of the spine.

Except for those of us who become astronauts, we can all expect to spend our lives, from our teen years onward, permanently losing some of the moisture from our discs. Because of the makeup of the disc's center, the balance gradually fails, and as some people know, we commonly lose an inch or more in height during our lifetime.

Whenever I describe this process to a group of back patients, somebody always asks why doctors can't do something to replace this lost moisture so as to maintain a person's discs at their original thickness. I point out that this is a natural process we're talking about here — not the onset of a disease. As we will see shortly, the drying-out process within the disc can cause trouble for some people, but in most cases it has the beneficial effect of stabilizing the spine. This is one reason why your back problems are likely to disappear as you grow old.

People also want to know why Nature picks on discs this way, causing them, of all body parts, to lose moisture. The answer to that loaded question is that discs are not exceptional in this respect. Many parts of your body lose moisture as you grow older. Your skin is an obvious example. It's easy to rejuvenate your skin with a little moisturizer, but we have no way of doing the same thing for your discs. Even a special diet will not alter this natural process.

As the center dries out, the disc flattens like a

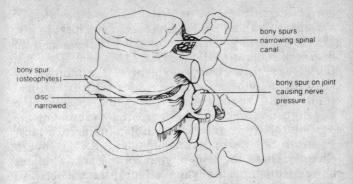

Fig. 10. Drying out of the disc allows the vertebrae to settle closer together. The nerve can be trapped between new bone growths on the rim of the facet joint and the edge of the vertebra. Misaligned by disc narrowing, the facet joints become worn.

dehydrated apricot; no longer is it the plumped-up cushion it once was. Some discs in your spine flatten more readily than others, if they are subjected to heavy physical stress. Because of the way your spine is curved, positioned, and structured, a few discs and vertebrae carry more of the load than others and are therefore most vulnerable. Basically, that's really all that goes wrong with discs — they dry out. But they retain their position and their basic structure. They do not disintegrate, turn to dust, or disappear. Just as the dried apricot is still the same fruit, the dehydrated disc remains an easily recognized part of your spine.

The Origins of Type One Pain

The loss of a bit of thickness in a disc — perhaps a quarter-inch or less — may not sound like much of a problem. But even that apparently minor loss can mean the difference between comfort and pain. For in its role as a shock-absorber, the disc must provide the proper amount of separation between the vertebrae above and below it. A reduction in the separation of vertebrae can create wear and tear on the facet joints. These joints are designed to work with a certain degree of separation. If the distance between the bones is decreased, the true alignment of the joint is destroyed. Imagine an electric motor with its central rotor out of alignment. As the motor operates, the misaligned rotor soon begins causing wear among the parts intended to interact with it. Similarly, a facet joint can fall victim to misalignment. As we saw in Chapter Three, the discs of your spine serve as buffers between other parts of your vertebrae but not between the bones of the facet joints. As a disc flattens, the two vertebrae come together and the "unbuffered" bones of the facet joint begin grinding against each other. It's not a pleasant ailment to have, but it's not a disease either — just a local, mechanical problem.

The grinding action is painful in itself, and soon the friction roughens those smooth surfaces that normally enable the joint to function so well. Thus, the malfunctioning joint compounds the pain you are already feeling from simple irritation. You now have a standard, bona fide case of Type One backache. And you have already seen how complications quickly set in from here on because of the connections with the local spinal nerve: after small-joint pain comes leg pain, then muscle spasm, then curvature to one side, then additional muscle spasm, and, finally, virtual immobility.

Meanwhile, back at the original trouble spot, your body reacts protectively by attempting to immobilize the painful area. The joint becomes inflamed, causing swelling, which limits movement but produces pain.

At this point, you may become vulnerable to a fearsome little game of Speaking Doctor, because an inflamed joint, as you know now, is called arthritis. For this type of inflammation due to wear and tear, the term is osteoarthritis. It's bad enough to have an inflamed joint, but when it's described as "osteo-arthritis of the spine" it sounds like a death sentence. Can't you just visualize your backbone turning to chalk? Yet some doctors, I'm sorry to say, use this term without explaining exactly what it means. If anybody plays this version of Speaking Doctor with you, remind yourself that you do not have a disease. No horrible infection has invaded your spine. When the irritation stops — and stop it will — the inflammation will clear up and the pain will subside.

The disc alone is not always to blame for facet pain. Sometimes wear and tear on the facet joint comes about simply through aging. The bones may grow brittle and become vulnerable to compression from weight on the spine. Or the body may fail to supply a facet joint with enough lubricating fluid. With those weaknesses present, any flattening of the disc will merely compound the problem.

Now that you have a clear picture of Type One backache and its causes, you can see why the pain is relieved when you bend forward. The forward position removes pressure from those bones at the very back of your spine, and the source of irritation is reduced temporarily. Conversely, any condition that forces you to arch your back — bad posture, pregnancy, a pot belly from overweight — will increase the pressure and aggravate the pain. Often, these additional conditions are erroneously blamed as the original causes of low-back pain. Fat people sometimes slim down in the belief that they can cure their back problems by losing weight. Inevitably they are disappointed, because weight loss, while removing one source of aggravation, does nothing to solve the problem of the worn facet.

If you are skeptical about the reason I have given for the relationship between the arching of your back due to bad posture, or whatever, and the intensifying of Type One pain, try this simple demonstration of a joint under stress. In this case it's your wrist joint

we're using as the example. First, make your right
hand into a fist and hold it out in front of you with the
knuckles facing away. Now, with your left hand slap
hard against the front of that fist. As you'll see, the
action causes stress but no discomfort in your right
wrist. Next, open your fist, straighten out your fingers
fully, and arch them back as far as you can, imitating
the way a traffic policeman signals an oncoming car to
stop. Now repeat the slapping motion, forcing the
fingers of your right hand back towards you. Immediately you feel pain in your wrist. The difference
between the two situations illustrates the difference
between a normal facet and a facet under increased
pressure. In the first instance, when you formed a fist,
your wrist joint was in "neutral," with enough "give"
to absorb the stress. In the second instance, with your
fingers bent fully backward, your wrist joint was held
in an extreme position, and the "give" was gone. The
result of the stress was immediate pain.

When a facet joint is worn and you arch your back,
the "give" is gone, and very little stress is needed to
cause pain. The simple act of stepping boldly off a curb
can be enough.

The Origins of Type Two Pain

Whenever a disc begins to flatten out, two other things
may go wrong. The disc itself may bulge out painfully
or it may press against a nerve.

Earlier, I likened a protruding disc to a tap washer
being squeezed out of shape under pressure, thus
bulging beyond its normal diameter. This happens as
the disc loses moisture and the vertebrae settle closer
together. This bulging might not be a problem if the
disc could feel no pain; its shell, however, is pain-
sensitive. If the bulging is gradual, the nerve ends
have a chance to conform, and the discomfort is no
greater than, say, the gradual bulging of your stomach
during a heavy meal. But if the bulge occurs suddenly,

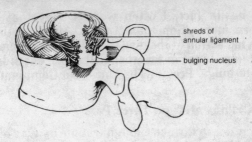

shreds of
annular ligament

bulging nucleus

Fig. 11. Protrusion of the disc nucleus usually occurs at the back corner of the disc, a naturally weak area in the outer shell.

perhaps because part of the shell gives way or tears open, the disc feels sudden, acute pain. When that happens, you have Type Two backache.

The location of this rapid bulging accounts for the way Type Two backache is aggravated when you bend forward. Whereas a painful facet joint, being located at the back of your spine, is aggravated when you bend back, a protruding disc, being further forward — located on the forward side of a pivot point — is squeezed by forward motion. It's like tightening down on that tap washer by giving the screw another turn.

As I mentioned earlier, the main nerve that supplies sensation to the facet joint is the same nerve that serves the disc. Consequently, Type Two backache touches off the same ugly sequence of pain radiation that we recited for Type One: local pain, leg pain, muscle spasm, unnatural curvature, more muscle spasm, immobility. By now the only noticeable difference between Types One and Two is that One is worse when you bend backward and Two is worse when you bend forward.

Unfortunately, there is no law to prevent you from having Type One and Type Two backache simultaneously or in succession, and if you do, you will display both of those bending symptoms, either at the same time or from one attack to the next, as the case may be. In fact, I often wonder why that doesn't happen more often than it does. After all, the same splaying action of the disc that allows the bones of the facet joint to grind together will cause one side of the disc to bulge. Presto! The One-Two Combination!

The Origins of Type Three Pain

As if it doesn't cause enough trouble by way of Types One and Two, the worn disc is also the culprit in Type Three backache — the pinched nerve. Once the center of the disc has lost moisture and allowed the bones to settle, the outer shell of the disc begins pushing outward. In this way, it can become directly or indirectly responsible for creating pressure on a nerve.

Before I explain how that happens, I want to interject a word about terminology, in case somebody baffles you by speaking Doctor about a disc. Throughout this book, I use the expressions "bulging disc" and "protruding disc" as interchangeable terms. I have chosen them because they are readily understood; they do not need to be defined because they are more or less self-explanatory. You may find, however, that your own doctor uses some other term to describe the same condition. He may say a disc is herniated, ruptured, prolapsed, cracked, fractured, or distended. They all mean the same thing. Or you may be told that a disc is sequestrated, which means that the bulging has developed to a point where a portion of the disc has torn loose. It's just a further stage of the same process.

As we saw in Chapter Three, one side of each disc is situated very close to the place where a main nerve branch leaves the spinal cord. Once that side of a disc has protruded even slightly, it can easily come into contact with the nerve. And only a slight degree of contact, in the form of touching, rubbing, or squeezing, can be enough to produce pain. That's the direct way in which a disc may place pressure on a nerve root.

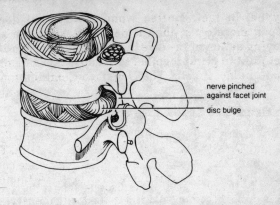

Fig. 12. A bulge at the back corner of the disc may squeeze the nerve root against the front of the facet joint. This type of direct pressure on the nerve is the least common of the three major causes of backache.

The disc's indirect involvement in pressure on a nerve occurs when the disc flattens out enough to permit the two vertebrae to come very close together. As we saw earlier, those nerve branches leave the spinal cord between every pair of vertebrae. Their points of exit are not holes in the bones, but spaces between the bones. When those spaces are reduced, the exiting nerve branch will be pinched. It is the bones, of course, that do the actual pinching, but the disc is the original culprit, for failing to hold the bones apart properly.

Those are the two conditions usually referred to as a pinched nerve, although the direct form of nerve pressure involves a rubbing or squeezing action rather than pinching.

How can you tell whether your pinched nerve (assuming you have one) is the result of direct contact between a disc and a nerve or the result of having a nerve pinched between adjacent vertebrae? The answer is that you can't, with any certainty. One useful clue, however, is your age. If you are under sixty and

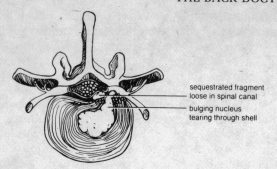

sequestrated fragment
loose in spinal canal
bulging nucleus
tearing through shell

Fig. 13. As the outer shell of the disc tears, the softer nucleus
bulges through, coming in direct contact with the nerve root.
In rare instances, a fragment of the nucleus may break loose
and lie free in the spinal canal.

have a pinched nerve, chances are you have a disc in
direct contact with a nerve. This condition, incidentally, is the much commoner of the two. If you are older
than sixty, it is likely that the nerve is being squeezed
between two vertebrae; older people are not usually
troubled by newly protruding discs.

The sequestrated disc, mentioned a few paragraphs
ago, is fairly rare among people with pinched nerves —
who, in turn, are only a small minority among people
with common backache. Even so, I have seen many
cases of sequestrated discs, and they can be tricky to
diagnose. Once that little piece of disc has torn loose
and become lodged in a nerve canal, a doctor can be
confused by the findings. The disc, having been
relieved of the pressure that caused it to bulge, now
emits very little pain. The severed fragment of disc,
having no nerve connections with the body, has no
feelings whatever. And the nerve being irritated by
the loose piece will exhibit symptoms similar to those
of simpler forms of back trouble. If the disc is lodged in
a nerve tunnel beneath a joint, for instance, the pain
will be aggravated when the person arches his back —
a symptom of Type One trouble — and yet there will be

evidence as well of nerve irritation — which is Type Three. When it comes to diagnosis, sequestrated discs are a challenge. They also belong to a small minority of back cases requiring surgery; the quickest way to stop that little piece of wandering disc from making trouble is to remove it by surgical methods.

Although I have emphasized that the pinched nerve is not necessarily more painful than Type One or Type Two backache, Type Three can certainly cause a lot of pain. I have especially vivid recollections of one unfortunate man, a clerical worker in his mid-forties, who swore that the only way he could be comfortable was on his hands and knees.

This man was already in hospital when I first saw him. He insisted on remaining on his hands and knees almost constantly. He stayed in bed on his hands and knees. He took his meals on his hands and knees. He moved to and from the bathroom on his hands and knees. All the staff on the ward regarded him as an eccentric. But, strange as it appeared, examination revealed findings that couldn't be ignored — signs the man couldn't fake if he tried. Only one conclusion made sense: like many people with Type Two or Type Three backache, this man had found he could relieve his pain by arching his back. And, because the pain was extremely intense, he remained on his hands and knees during every possible moment, allowing gravity to keep his back arched for him. In fact, we found that the man had a protruding disc with nerve pressure — a condition that could be remedied by surgery. We operated, and he was relieved of his backache.

When there is irritation to a nerve, the pain flashes along the length of the nerve branch and all its tributaries. This gives the impression that some of the pain is originating in other parts of the body served by that nerve branch, such as the thighs or lower legs. All three kinds of common back pain can produce this picture, but only with Type Three backache is the problem actually due to pressure on a nerve. The tests for direct nerve irritation setout in Chapter Four (pages 62–65) is designed to determine whether this is in fact what is happening.

With the nerve impulses blocked at one point, the signals are scrambled all along the nerve. The orderly functions of the nerve are disrupted, and the effects are felt right to the boundaries of the system. You lose control of the muscles out there, the responses we call reflexes are blocked off, and you can no longer receive sensory reports from down the line. That is why we were able to say in the previous chapter that you probably don't have Type Three pain with nerve damage if you can pass the muscular test (standing on tiptoe and walking on your heels), the reflex test (knees and ankles), and the sensory test (pricking your calves and both sides of your feet).

Before you drop this book in fright, convinced that you have Type Three back trouble about to shut down your entire nervous system, I must make several important points. Not only is Type Three backache — direct pressure on a nerve — uncommon, but even when it does occur, the pressure is usually so slight that it causes pain from direct nerve irritation without any loss of function. In other words, there is no loss of muscle power, reflexes, or sensation. Finally, in the occasional instance where nerve pressure is long enough and strong enough to disrupt the signals, loss of function happens in only one nerve, supplying, at most, a few muscles or a small area of sensation. The result is serious and may have a profound effect on one movement in the leg or the foot, but it can never cause widespread paralysis.

Now, if you have been reading this explanation with a skeptical attitude, you may be saying to yourself, "Well, he makes that sound all very neat and tidy, but how can he assume that the pinched nerve will affect my lower legs and feet? Don't I have other nerve branches running to other parts of my legs and the rest of my body? Couldn't my pinched nerve — assuming I have one — happen to be a nerve that affects, say, my knee or my hip or even my belly button?"

The answer is, yes, it is possible — but unlikely. Again I'm working on the principle that common things happen most commonly.

First of all, as I implied at the beginning of this chapter, as your spine begins to feel the effects of constant use and gradual aging, the spots under heavy stress become particularly vulnerable to trouble. All discs will lose moisture and become flatter than normal, but the real trouble-makers will be the discs that are under heavy mechanical stress.

Back specialists know from experience that, because of this stress factor, three discs in your spine are far more likely to cause trouble than all the others combined. One of these is a disc in your neck — the C_{5-6}. It causes problems similar to those that develop in the low back, but only about half as often. Statistically, the great preponderance of trouble comes from two discs in your low back — the L_{4-5} and the L_5-S_1. These are the discs that affect the nerves running into your lower legs and feet — which explains the rationale for the nerve tests in Chapter Four. These two levels alone account for ninety percent of all low-back pain. And if you include the disc directly above, namely the L_{3-4} (which affects the nerve supplying the knee reflex and the ability to feel on the inside of your calves), we're talking about the sources of ninety-six percent of all disc problems causing pain in the low back.

In other words, if you have disc problems in your low back affecting your nervous system, there is a ninety-six-percent chance that the symptoms will show up in your lower legs and feet.

Now that you know how each of the three types of common back pain develops, see what you can make of this unusual case, which I once had to diagnose and treat.

Scene I: A new patient, a matronly woman I'll call

Frances Jones, comes to see me with a familiar story. She has a lingering ache in her low back. The pain is not as acute as it once was, but it has persisted for several weeks. She feels pain as well in her buttock and down the back of her legs as far as the knees. By questioning and examining her, I learn that her leg and foot muscles are normal, and so are her knee and ankle reflexes and her ability to sense pain from pinpricks in her calves and feet. When she bends forward, her backache is worse.

What's wrong with Frances Jones? If you remember the descriptions in Chapter Four, you'll have no trouble identifying her problem as Type Two backache — the protruding disc.

At the time, I make the diagnosis and prescribe appropriate treatment, and Frances Jones's back pain subsides.

Scene II: Six months later. Frances Jones returns to my office with a new attack of backache. She tells me the old pain reappeared but then disappeared suddenly as a new pain developed in her right buttock. In some respects it sounds like the same old problem, but I soon find significant differences from the last attack. She now has pain the full length of her right leg and into her toes. Her right ankle reflex is gone, and she has lost the ability to feel pinpricks on the outside edge of her foot.

What's going on here? This is a patient who had Type Two backache, which has disappeared. Everything now points to Type Three. Additional testing tends to confirm my suspicions: her Type Two problem must have ended abruptly because the protruding portion of the disc tore loose, releasing pressure on the disc, just the way a weak spot on a tire will bulge out and then pop. That would account for the sudden cessation of pain. But how do we account for the Type Three pain that immediately followed? That fragment of disc which broke free lodged against a nerve and produced Type Three symptoms and findings.

The solution? Surgery. In the operating room I extract that wayward bit of disc from Frances Jones's back. Her problem is solved, and she recovers quickly.

Scene III: Another eighteen months have elapsed. Guess who is in my office again, complaining of terrible back pain. Is it another protruding disc? Another wandering fragment? Neither. Frances Jones presents me with a whole new set of symptoms and findings. By now I know her well enough to believe she is not exaggerating or faking. And so I'm fascinated to check out her condition. Her low-back pain is radiating into her buttocks and upper legs only. No signs of Type Three nerve problems. I rule out the recurrence of Type Two as well, because bending forward is not especially painful for her. In fact, it seems to relieve the pain. And that's the tipoff: arching her back is what hurts most. Frances Jones, having rid herself of Type Two and Type Three backache in that order, has come down with an unmistakable case of Type One!

Now that hardly seems fair, does it? And yet it's easy to understand, once you know the mechanics of common backache. The very same disc that had caused Type Two pain during its protruding period and Type Three during its "wandering fragment" period is now indirectly to blame for the Type One pain. In flattening out, the disc has permitted the adjacent bones of the facet joints to come together and begin grinding painfully against each other.

Fortunately, by the time of this visit Frances Jones has acquired enough understanding of spinal anatomy to accept my explanation and follow my prescription of proper bed rest, strengthening exercises, and improved postural habits. Frances improved rapidly, and as far as I know she is still living normally, free of serious back problems, old or new. If she weren't, I expect I'd be the first to hear about it.

As tricky as cases like hers can be, they do not support the idea of the back as a medical mystery. I am convinced that any back problem, however complex

and puzzling, can be correctly diagnosed and treated
Any back specialist can do it, given the experience, the
necessary determination, and full co-operation from
his patient.

Mind you, I'm not suggesting that the medical world
knows everything there is to know about the human
back and what ails it. Certainly there are important
facts yet to be determined and questions still to be
answered. For instance, why do worn joints hurt?
Nobody knows. What is it about discs that causes
them to lose moisture? That is something no one can
explain. What mechanism of pain operates when a disc
touches a nerve? Experiments have proved that pressure alone is not the answer; the full explanation
remains to be found. And what about the relationship
between wear and tear and mechanical stress? Is wear
and tear the result of increased activity, or does it just
become more significant in active situations? Again
nobody has the answers.

My belief is that, as discussed earlier, wear and tear
is a normal development through late middle age
Some years ago, much was made of the fact that soon
after farm tractors came equipped with headlights
numerous farmers began suffering from a "new"
ailment dubbed "tractor back." Actually, it was just
good old common backache created in new circumstances. Headlights had made it possible for a man to
plow day and night — twice as long as before. But, in
my view, the mere act of sitting on a tractor seat never
gave anybody serious back trouble, any more than you
could say that the headlights themselves had caused
all that back pain. The longer work day simply created
unusually prolonged stress, which made normal wear
and tear painfully evident.

There is no doubt that certain occupations suffer a
higher incidence of back problems. Scientific studies
have found a greater-than-average occurrence of back
pain in miners, foundry workers, and stevedores. The

problem lies in trying to place the cart and the horse: does the increased amount of back pain reflect a real acceleration of the natural aging process from very heavy work, or does work requiring heavy lifting in awkward positions just accentuate normal backache?

One patient I examined who could lay claim to wearing out his back simply through hard work was a blacksmith. Yes, there are still a few blacksmiths around, working for riding academies and racing stables. This blacksmith was thirty-two years old when I saw him, and he had been shoeing horses since he was ten. In his adult years he worked twelve hours a day at his heavy tasks. Each time he fitted a shoe, he had to bend over at the waist, hold the weight of the horse's hoof and leg in a steady position, and swing a heavy hammer. X-rays showed his back to be in a condition of wear and tear that might be expected in a man twice his age. No wonder his back was sore. He could truthfully say he had worn it out through hard work. Few of us can make that claim, no matter what we do for a living or how hard we work.

The encouraging aspect of this story is that even though he has literally worn out his back, that black-smith is not prevented from doing anything he wants to do. Not even his job. Wear and tear has not made his work impossible — just more difficult. Like everyone else with common backache, he can look forward to having his condition improve with age. Meanwhile, he has cut his work day in half. I put him on a program of abdominal exercise and helped him find ways of modifying his non-working activities, to give his back plenty of rest between work sessions.

The real-life case of the blacksmith's backache brings up two fundamental points — points on which this book is based. One point is that bad backs tend to repair themselves. As I said in an earlier chapter (page 11), while no one can predict what will become of any individual's condition as a result of aging, statistics show that back pain is most common in the middle years. Backs improve by regaining stability. A disc will shrink only so far, and then it will become stable in the new position. Your spine will become shorter; hence the loss of height as you grow old. Meanwhile, your spine will grow projections — bone spurs — around a disc, to help stabilize it. In other words, contrary to popular notion, bone spurs are not a source of trouble; rather, they are an aid in the solution. Another aspect of the same repair process is the fact that your facet joints will reshape themselves to accommodate their new position, eliminating the increased pressure and allowing room for the nerves to pass by.

The other point is that nearly all the things that need to be done to control your back in the meantime are things you can do for yourself.

Many of my patients are skeptical the first time they are told these facts. They have always assumed that once anybody has a bad back, it will become progressively worse right on into old age. Yet, as we all know, as you move into those so-called senior years — from, say, age sixty-five onward — your back stiffens up; everybody's does, whether there has been pain or not. And once your back is less mobile, doing less twisting and bending, its sore spots and weaknesses become less subject to strain. New mechanical back trouble is uncommon after sixty-five. (The elderly are susceptible to backache from some of the causes described in the next section of this chapter, but these are not mechanical conditions, and they are quite rare.)

My patients have to be convinced as well that the body's marvelous self-repairing process will go to work immediately on any back that is given proper rest. That's hard advice to take, I know, especially when the pain is at its peak; people want something dramatic done for them. But bed rest is usually the best treatment at that point, just the same. Knowing this can be a great comfort — and a great aid to healing.

The Rarer Causes of Back Pain

Now that I have concentrated so long on the sources, symptoms, and causes of common backache, you may be wondering if I ever concern myself with any other kinds of back pain. The answer is that in my professional work I am concerned with the whole range of back problems. To cover them all in detail, however, would require a book many times the size of this one, and few readers would find the additional information useful. Such a book would include ailments so rare that not one person in a thousand ever encounters them. Collectively, these diseases account for no more than ten percent of all back complaints. And even the victims of those rare ailments would gain little from reading about them, for they are beyond the realm of self-help.

If you have symptoms that do not correspond with any that I have described for common back pain, I suggest that you ask your doctor for a thorough examination.

Even if you feel sure that your back trouble is one of the common types, you may find it useful to learn a little about the rarer causes, since you may need to distinguish these from certain conditions of common backache that masquerade under impressive-sounding names such as "osteoarthritis of the spine," which, as we saw earlier, is nothing more than an inflamed facet joint.

Here, then, are brief descriptions of some rarer forms of backache you may hear about.

Ankylosing Spondylitis

Primarily a young man's disease, ankylosing spondylitis causes widespread, acute inflammation of the spinal joints and can also affect the hips and knees. Of unknown cause, it is characterized by a visible flattening of the surface of the low back, a loss of chest movement, and marked stiffness of the spinal joints.

For some reason, ankylosing spondylitis occurs slightly more often in Britain than in North America. As it progresses, the disease stiffens the back by fusing all the vertebrae together. The disease may arrest itself spontaneously at any time.

The pain of the acute inflammation can be relieved by anti-inflammatory drugs. Proper treatment must include instruction in appropriate postural habits, such as sleeping without a pillow, so that as the spine becomes fused, it will be fused in its optimum position. Established deformities may require major spinal surgery.

Cancers of the Spine — Primary

These extremely rare diseases may result from cancerous growths in the vertebrae, the bone marrow, the nerves, the muscles, or the fibrous tissues of the spine. Characterized by local tenderness and local pain unaffected by rest or exercise, primary cancer of the spine can usually be detected by bone-scan techniques, X-ray, or blood tests.

Any or all of three forms of treatment may be used: drug therapy, radiotherapy (that is, X-ray), and surgery.

Cancers of the Spine — Secondary

Though more common than primary cancers of the spine, these conditions are still relatively rare. The term "secondary" means that the cancer has originated elsewhere in the body, often in the lungs, the breast, or the prostate gland, and then spread to the spine. A person who has back pain as well as cancer in some other part of the body need not assume, however, that the back pain is a symptom of secondary spinal cancer. It is quite possible that ordinary wear and tear, unrelated to the cancer, is causing common backache.

Treatment of secondary cancer of the spine is the

same as for primary cancer and can be carried out simultaneously with treatment at the primary site of the disease. Since cancers of the breast and the prostate gland are dependent on hormones, treatment in such cases is likely to involve hormonal therapy.

Osteoporosis

In this condition, which occurs in later years, the bones of the back become abnormally thin and thus vulnerable to fracture and compression. One cause of osteoporosis is disuse — typically, in a person confined to bed for a long period without exercise. A more generalized form of the disease, arising from causes still unknown, affects all the body but primarily the spine. The victims of this form are most often women who have passed menopause. According to one widely held theory, the problem arises from the loss of the hormone estrogen, without which the bones become abnormally thin.

The most common symptom of osteoporosis is a sudden back pain immediately following a minor injury that causes a vertebral fracture. The pain of the fracture gradually disappears, but if there are repeated traumas, mechanical problems may arise from altered alignment of the vertebrae, creating a hunched back.

Treatment of the pain and the mechanical problems is the same as for common backache. Control of the osteoporosis itself can sometimes be achieved through the use of hormones, vitamin D, or chemicals such as fluoride — the material also used to prevent tooth decay. Post-menopausal women who have this disease may be given estrogen, which sometimes helps to restore normal bone density.

Paget's Disease

With this affliction, repeated episodes of bone destruction occur throughout the body, including the spine. These episodes are followed each time by repeated attempts at natural bone repair. The cause is unknown. The effect of these alternating processes may be excessive growth of bone, which consequently presses on one or more nerves, or it may be destruction of the vertebrae through compression.

Paget's Disease is rarely seen before the age of forty. When extensive, it gives the victim a dwarf or gnome-like appearance, with a large head and rounded shoulders. Experiments are under way to retard this excessive bone reaction by means of chemicals.

Rheumatoid Arthritis

Of all the musculoskeletal diseases affecting people in North America and the United Kingdom, this is the largest single crippler. Definite rheumatoid arthritis affects one percent of the population, while some features of the disease afflict another two percent.

A person with rheumatoid arthritis will typically suffer inflammation of many joints of the body, including those of the spine. Diagnosis will be confirmed by blood tests and X-rays showing a typical pattern of joint destruction. When the spine is affected, the problem is usually centered in the neck rather than in the low back.

Treatment may be medical or surgical. Aspirin is the drug of choice. Other medications may include gold, chloroquine, indomethacin, and steroids. Surgery may be undertaken to repair or replace the joints. General treatment includes physiotherapy involving proper rest, exercise, and the adoption of proper postural habits.

According to the American Rheumatism Association, out of every twenty patients suffering from rheumatoid arthritis, five recover completely and five others experience complete healing with residual (but usually minor) deformities.

Scheuermann's Disease

Some people know this affliction as Juvenile Round-back, so called because its victims, typically between eleven and fourteen years of age, have backs with a pronounced forward curve. This condition results from a defect in the normal growth of the vertebrae, which become wedged-shaped instead of drum-like. The cause of this defect is not known.

Minor cases can be treated by physiotherapy to improve posture, and, during the growing years, by the application of a brace. Severe cases in adults may require surgery to straighten the spine.

Scoliosis

The most notorious victim of scoliosis, at least in fiction, was Victor Hugo's Hunchback of Notre Dame. Fortunately, few cases of scoliosis are that extreme. A typical case is characterized by an abnormal curve in the spine, a slight hump, and a less obvious protrusion of one side of the chest. The condition, which afflicts girls more often than boys, begins during growth, with the spine twisting and curving to one side. Most scoliosis occurs in the upper back, and the cause is unknown, although we suspect genetic factors play a part. Scoliosis may also result from congenital defor-mities, trauma, chest surgery, or muscular imbalance caused by paralytic disease.

During growth, a patient can be treated with exer-cise and bracing. In an adult, severe curves can be corrected only by surgery. Scoliosis affecting the low back may be associated with common backache. The more typical upper-back curve is usually pain-free.

Many schools throughout North America operate screening programs to detect scoliosis in their stu-dents. When detection is early, between the ages of eleven and fourteen, management is most effective.

About fifteen percent of the population have scoliosis, but most cases are so slight that its victims
are unaware of their condition, and no treatment is
required.

Spina Bifida

I include spina bifida in this list only because so many
people believe it is a cause of back pain. This belief is
based on a common misuse of the term, since spina
bifida, as such, is neither painful nor serious. There is
a more extreme form of the same condition, but it is
very rare and is given a separate name. Early in our
embryo stage, the spine and the nervous system are in
the form of two flat layers covering the back. As the
embryo grows, the layers curve into two tubes, one
inside the other. Sometimes the outer tube, which will
form the bone, fails to close, leaving a gap through
which the inner tube, now the nervous system, is
exposed. Extreme cases are obvious at birth because
the defect allows the infant's spinal cord and nerves to
protrude under the skin. This condition is called
meningomyelocoele. Cases of spina bifida typically
involve only one vertebra, with a gap in its posterior
elements so narrow — one or two millimeters — that its
existence is discovered by chance, years later, when
the spine is X-rayed for some other reason. The gap is
full of thick, fibrous tissue, and the spine is functional-
ly normal. This minor X-ray defect is termed spina
bifida and is not a cause of back pain.

Spondylitis

This disease, an inflammatory condition of the spine,
may arise from infection or chemical reaction. If it is
produced by a bacterial infection it is sometimes
called osteomyelitis of the spine. Chemical irritation
may occur as a result of tests, such as discography,
conducted to diagnose back pain. Infection may result

from surgery, open-back injury, or an infection that spreads to the spine from elsewhere in the body.

Whatever the source of trouble, the inflammation is usually treated with antibiotics, rest, and sometimes a brace or cast to immobilize the spine. Rarely, surgery will be undertaken to drain the infection or decompress or fuse the affected segment.

Spondylolisthesis

This is not a disease but a mechanical condition in which one vertebra slips over another. This may happen for any of five reasons: a defect within the interlocking joint system at the back of the spine (a condition called spondylolysis, which is described below); a congenital abnormality in the design of a facet joint; an advanced case of wear in a set of facet joints; a major trauma; or a bone ailment, such as Paget's Disease, which changes the shape of the bone.

In adolescents, surgery may be required to restore the vertebra to its proper position. In adults, minor cases of spondylolisthesis are treated like common backache. Severe slips may require surgery to prevent further shifting.

Spondylolysis

Not to be confused with spondylolisthesis — though it often is, even by doctors — spondylolysis is a defect in the posterior portion of a vertebra, usually one in the low back. Although its cause is not certain, it is thought to result from a fracture in early childhood (before age five), a fracture that fails to heal. The result is an abnormal separation between the upper and lower sets of vertebral joints. Intermittent back pain is the typical symptom. Although spondylolysis may cause slippage of the affected vertebra (spondylolisthesis), this complication is by no means inevitable. Nor does the unmended break necessarily cause common backache. The incidence of spondylolysis in the population at large is about ten percent. Among the Inuit of Baffin Island, in the Canadian Arctic, the incidence is fifty percent, perhaps because youngsters there are habitually falling on the ice.

Throughout this book I am assuming that you, the reader, have none of the rare afflictions listed here but are suffering instead from common backache. It's a reasonably safe assumption, and if it's correct, I can assure you that not only have you a lot of company but also you are one of the lucky ones — if anyone with back pain can be called lucky. For while it is not my intention to dissuade anyone from seeing a doctor, I want to make it clear to you that the self-help procedures set out in this book may be all the treatment and therapy you will need to bring your back trouble under control for the rest of your life.

6 Is It All in Your Head?

I have seen unusual back patients in my day but none more bizarre than a man I'll call Ralph Rogers.

In his later thirties, Rogers suffered from common backache, which he relieved by lying in bed day after day. Nothing bizarre about that. But Rogers, you see, was a professional writer, and by the time I saw him he had become obsessed with his problem and with the need to go right on working in bed — typewriter and all. He had designed and built an elaborate frame on which he suspended his typewriter over his bed so that he could somehow manage to write while flat on his back.

Although I never saw his contraption, I could tell by the way he described it that he had put a great deal of thought and effort into its design and construction. If he had devoted even half as much time and energy to back exercise and care, he could have been leading a normal life by this time, with little or no pain.

Obviously, that was not what he wanted. He was inordinately proud of his invention and content with his self-appointed role as a bed-ridden martyr with an incurable illness.

I don't know why Ralph Rogers came to see me, unless it was to gain medical approval of his ridiculous "solution" to a routine problem. In any case, the moment I suggested a more rational approach, I lost him as a patient. I never saw him again, but he has remained in my memory as one extraordinary example of how a person's emotional response to back trouble can shut out any attempt at sensible treatment.

Even among back patients who respond more moderately to pain than Ralph Rogers did, there is always an important emotional element that must be considered along with the physical. Previous chapters have offered a thorough grounding in the physical aspects. Now it's time to gain a clear understanding of the role your emotions play in making your back ache.

Most people, I think, recognize that there is a close relationship between mind and body. They know, for instance, that physical illness can readily cause an emotional upset, and that a positive emotional response can play an important part in warding off an illness or bringing about a speedy recovery. But I have found that many people with back problems do not realize, or will not acknowledge, the extent to which their emotions can contribute to their pain.

When you feel a twinge of back pain, your first reaction may be physical, in the form of muscle spasm. Or it may be emotional, in the form of anxiety or fear. The nature of your emotional response depends on your personality, but regardless of the type of person you are, there is always a response. Chronic back pain is never just a physical problem. Your emotional response, though not necessarily thought out in words, may amount to something as simple and obvious as "Look out — here comes a new attack of back pain!" That emotion, in turn, will trigger a muscle spasm, which produces pain. The pain triggers more muscle spasms and more anxiety. And so it goes — not around in a circle but in a downward spiral, with the physical and emotional elements becoming more intense at every round.

This pattern is not peculiar to backache, by any means. Worry can aggravate almost any physical illness, and vice versa. Feelings of depression are a common reaction to heart problems, for instance, and they can be so inhibiting to recovery that some heart specialists refuse to risk surgery while a patient's morale is low. I am convinced, however, that the emotional element is even more destructive in back pain than in other illnesses because those myths and misconceptions we discussed in Chapter One generate fears and anxieties far out of proportion to the actual physical problem. Such emotions can become powerful and destructive forces in our lives — if we let them.

Emotion can cause physical illness, as we've already seen in the description of muscle spasm as a reaction to anxiety. Emotion can determine our reaction to illness. Witness our bed-ridden friend with the typewriter. Emotion can influence the way we follow a doctor's advice. ("He told me to get up on the fifth day, but I was afraid of hurting my back again. So I stayed in bed for the rest of the month.") Emotion can prolong our symptoms. I have many patients whose bodies have memorized old pain and continue feeling it long after the original physical condition has ceased to be the cause.

Emotional tension can bring on an attack identical to the original physical episode. I can testify to that phenomenon from personal experience. Several years ago I was teaching my young daughter how to do somersaults. I discovered it is impossible to describe a somersault to a six-year-old and expect to be understood: I had to perform a demonstration. In the course of doing just two somersaults, I wrenched my neck and developed an acute attack of facet pain. The pain subsided rapidly, as I expected, and I had forgotten the episode when, three months later, I was performing a very difficult operation. As the tension mounted, the neck pain suddenly reappeared. It was identical to the pain I had suffered while somersaulting. I hadn't reinjured my neck: I was just suffering emotional tension. The moment the operation ended — successfully — my neck pain disappeared. I had experienced a textbook example of memorized pain.

The key to controlling negative emotions is understanding. Without knowing you personally I could not predict your emotional reactions to backache — or any

other illness — because we all respond in our own
way. When two people suffer broken legs, one may go
into a state of depression and stare at the wall for
hours, while the other uses his enforced spare time to
call old friends or catch up on his reading. There are,
however, certain interactions of mind and body that
are common to us all, and by understanding them you
can begin to explore your individual emotional re
sponses to backache.

First, let's see how emotional stress can aggravate
physical pain. This can happen in three ways, which
sum up as "tension," "focus," and "body language."

Tension is a normal condition; your muscles
couldn't function without it. But sometimes it occurs
for emotional reasons. If those emotional feelings
remain unexpressed and unreleased, the tension per
sists. Prolonged tension produces pain.

Suppose, for example, that you have an argument
with your spouse at breakfast. You become angry.
Your stomach churns. Your jaws clench. The muscles
in your neck, shoulders, and back tighten up. That
tension may remain throughout the day. By late
afternoon you may have forgotten all about the argu
ment, but your body hasn't. And that tension is now
producing pain. An early-morning argument has be
come literally a pain in the neck and you don't even
realize the connection. If you happen to be one of the
millions of people with worn facet joints or protruding
discs, that's where you'll feel the discomfort most. You
could be in for a dandy bout of back trouble.

Focus is the term many of us use to describe the
process of concentration. Routinely our minds screen
out many impulses that constantly bombard our
senses. This enables us to concentrate on whatever is
important to us at the moment. If you are sitting at a
public meeting, listening to a good speaker at the front
of the hall, your mind will focus your attention so that
you become oblivious to the hardness of the auditori-

um chair, the humming of the ventilation system, the glare of the ceiling lights, or the whiff of the cigar two rows back. If the speaker is very good, your focus may be so strong that almost nothing will disrupt your concentration. That's a useful form of focus.

Sometimes, however, we are inclined to focus our attention on pain. Soon we become conscious of it to the exclusion of everything else. It's like running your tongue over a tooth cavity even when you know the action will hurt. The more we focus on pain, the more we feel it. And pain is a spell-binding speaker.

You can avoid this hazard, however, by adopting techniques set out in a later chapter of this book — exercises and postural habits that become second nature and pleasant substitutes for the destructive practice of focusing on pain.

Body language is an unconscious means we all use to express feelings we can't put into words. Watch somebody unconsciously nod her head as she listens to a person with whom she agrees. Notice the erect, shoulder-back posture of the man who just got the raise he knew he deserved. Observe the dejected slump of the clerk at his desk who has just been told that after a week's effort the accounts don't balance. Those are all instances of body language that everybody can recognize.

A housewife has had a rough day at home with the children. Her husband comes home and sits down to read the paper. She feels a strong need to tell somebody how tired and discouraged she is, but he doesn't seem interested. She decides not to bring up the subject. As she represses her feelings, her body begins expressing them for her, by tensing up and developing pain. Although she doesn't realize what's happening, she's finding another way, through her body, of saying, "Hey — I've had a bad day." If the pain happens to develop where her spine has already suffered some wear and tear, she could be in for several days of backache. Had this woman realized how the repression of her feelings would affect her, she would probably have made the effort to express those feelings more directly.

Physical pain is capable of generating a wide range of emotional responses. An attack of back pain, especially, can generate fear, anxiety, panic, hysteria, despair, depression, frustration, hopelessness, guilt, inadequacy, a sense of failure — or almost any combination of those emotions.

Not long ago I examined a man who had already been referred to physiotherapy by his family doctor. By his manner and the expression on his face I could see that he was frightened out of his wits. When I asked him what was bothering him, he showed me a slip of paper he had in his wallet. It was the requisition his doctor had made out for the physiotherapist. The man had just spent a considerable amount of time listening to his doctor describe what he had found wrong with the man's back. Throughout the explanation, the doctor had emphasized repeatedly that the problem was not serious and was not a disease. But when the patient read the requisition, he found a term that seemed to contradict everything the doctor had said. It read "osteoarthritis." One fearful and misleading phrase had been enough to touch off an emotional reaction that could do untold damage to the man's morale — and aggravate his back pain tremendously.

In a more typical incident not long ago, a woman came to our Back Education Unit in a bad state of fright. Her doctor had told her she had several slipped discs. She believed that any violent movement could cause her spine to collapse into a pile of bones. I'm sure that until she learned the facts about her condition, that poor woman suffered more from fear than from backache.

One emotional response often generates many others. A fearful person may grow panicky and withdraw from all activity: no work, no recreation, no sexual relations. In the extreme, the person may suffer financially and socially, with less income and few associations with friends — conditions that touch off feelings of inadequacy, loneliness, self-doubt, and concern over money. Sexual restraint produces feelings of insufficiency on the part of the backache victim, resentment on the part of the partner, and frustration for both.

Emotional responses may not be triggered by a single, acute attack, but they are almost inevitable with chronic trouble, by which I mean either a persistent backache or a series of repeated attacks with perhaps only short periods of relief between them. Chronic backache is especially conducive to depression because the pain gives you the feeling that your normal life is over and that you will be suffering this way for the rest of your life.

The difference between a manageable attack and an unmanageable chronic condition is like the difference between physical punishment and random torture. A person sentenced to a clearly defined form of corporal punishment can brace himself for it, endure it, and begin to recover. The agony is a thousand times worse for the prisoner who has no idea when the goons will show up at his cell door, how severe the next session will be, or how long it will last. Worst of all, he can't help fearing that his ordeal will go on for the rest of his life. You may identify readily with that second situation if the back-pain goons have been at your door.

There is no need, of course, for you to undergo such psychological torture. You can learn to live with your condition without having to live with the pain or suffer the anticipation of a severe attack. It's within your power to banish virtually all those emotional responses by learning to cope with any attack of pain. Once you get to know your back and understand how resistant it is to real damage, and once you master the techniques of relieving the acute pains that may occur, you are on your way to winning the psychological side of the battle.

Just as your mind and your body react in the production of pain, so you and your family can interact in ways that aggravate your condition. Your family may do you — and themselves — a disservice by showing either too much concern about your back problems, or too little.

Over-concern, ironically, is a big danger for the person who is the ever-reliable "pillar of the family." I sometimes describe it as the Iron Housewife Syndrome, because it so often affects wives and mothers who have spent years serving their families without letup — never sick, never taking a day off, always on hand to cook the turkey on Christmas Day, always the one who cleans up the mess afterwards.

Housewives, of course, are not the only ones who find themselves in situations of this kind. This phenomenon affects people of both sexes. I think of it as the Iron Housewife Syndrome because it is imposed most often upon females who are the "anchorpersons" of their households. Marriage and gender have little to do with it except that they are part of the circumstances in which a person is expected to behave as though she were indestructible. Cast in this role, anyone — male or female, married or unmarried — is likely to respond in the same way to a sudden attack of back pain. The attack may be entirely physical at the outset, but the Iron Housewife immediately has a new need: the need to express her fear of what's wrong. Yet she has never felt comfortable showing any weakness. She can't talk about this feeling and she can't dismiss it. Her solution, to the surprise and alarm of her family, is to collapse into complete immobility.

The family rallies around her, convinced that whatever is wrong must be terribly serious because Good Old Mother would never let a minor back ailment slow her down. Now Mother is on the spot. Subconsciously she has to live up to her family's new expectations. The only way to do that is to suffer intense pain. Can you think of a more unpleasant way to get that message across?

As a back doctor, I often have great difficulty with this all-too-common occurrence, because I'm faced with the task of trying to make Mother and her family understand the real problem of her backache. Certainly her problem is physical — or at least it was at the beginning. But I have to convince everyone that the major, lasting disability is largely emotional.

"Never!" says the family. "Mother has always been the best worker we know. Magnifying her problem? Rubbish!"

Usually my comments are interpreted to mean that Mother is mentally unbalanced and that I am dismissing her pain as unreal.

Of course the pain is real. No one, least of all someone who is familiar with back pain, would ever suggest that the pain isn't real, or that it isn't as intense as Mother and her family say it is. Mother isn't a liar and she isn't faking the attacks. But the problem is not in her back as much as in her body's unexpected and devastating response to the pain. I always find that a hard message to get across, especially to a family convinced that either I don't understand the seriousness of the problem, or I have no compassion for the stricken patient.

Ironically, the same emotional response — subconsciously intensified pain — can also occur if a family displays too little concern for a backache victim's problems. When back pain strikes, the victim needs attention. If the family seems indifferent, the victim may be too considerate or too proud to demand attention in so many words. And so the body makes the demand instead, by producing a convincing degree of pain. The message is, "See, I really am in agony. Now everyone has to notice me."

Like anyone else, you could be the victim of over-concern or under-concern on the part of the people around you — and not necessarily your family. It could happen to you at work. If you have been playing the role of Reliable Charlie — never late, never off sick, always there when needed — you may have set yourself up as a victim of over-concern on the part of your colleagues. Or, if your role is less conspicuous, you could suffer from indifference from the people at work. Either way, your back pain will undergo some unnecessary aggravation.

Both situations can lead to the same reaction. As you subconsciously prolong your pain, your family or colleagues grow suspicious: "Are you sure it isn't all in your head?" By now, there is no way that words can prove what you know is true. The only convincing response must come from your body — in the production of more pain. Your body can't allow you to get well without making you look like a phony.

You have to remember that these reactions take place outside your conscious control. Your mind and your back simply gang up on you to get what they want — more attention, more rest, more help. But you pay the price in continuing back pain.

As you have probably surmised by now, you can avoid the hazards of over-concern and under-concern by understanding these emotional processes in advance. Once you are aware of them, you will see the value in expressing yourself directly and clearly, so that your body will not have to convey your message by producing pain.

What we are talking about here, essentially, is the danger of becoming dependent on your pain. If you allow this to happen, your pain can become an indispensable part of your life. Dependency on illness, and on pain itself as proof of that illness, figure all too often in the lives of back patients, who could otherwise recover swiftly. It happens, often undetected, in private relationships, and it happens more visibly — at least from my vantage-point — to people who claim workers' compensation or accident-insurance payments, or both, or who enter into litigation over back injuries.

One situation I know of involves a patient of mine, a young homosexual who lives with a middle-aged woman. The woman provides him not only with room and board but also with the mothering he never had as a boy. What is she so solicitous? The poor young man has a bad back. As long as his back continues to produce pain, he has a meal ticket and the freedom to come and go as he pleases. He's paying a heavy price in pain, but you can imagine how he would resist any effort to make his back feel better.

I have another male patient, this one a young macho who insists he was on his way to becoming a professional hockey star until he developed back trouble. This man truly believes that only because of his back did he fail to achieve a career as a successful athlete. Actually, my patient tried out for the team he wanted to join, couldn't make the grade, and then developed back trouble. Now he's stuck with back pain as his permanent excuse for not being another Gordie Howe.

You may thing these people are malingering, but I can assure you they are not. I have examined these two young men, and many others like them, and I know their pain is real. It may not arise in their facet joints or discs, but by the time it registers in their consciousness as back pain, it hurts just the same.

The difference between malingering and using real pain in role-playing is the difference between telling a lie and living an unhappy truth. I like to illustrate that important difference with the analogy of the flooded basement. Suppose an acquaintance calls up and wants to come over to your house. You don't want him to visit but you are too polite to say so. Instead, you make up an excuse; you tell him you're in a crisis — the basement is flooded. You're lying, but you expect to get away with that story. That's malingering. Now suppose, instead, that you tell the same story and then feel compelled to hurry downstairs and flood your basement, just to make your story true. That, in effect, is what your subconscious does when it uses back pain to enable you to play a role. The big drawback, of course, is that you now have to cope with that basement full of water — or live with that aching back.

If you have had backache for a considerable time, it might pay you to examine your motives, privately and honestly, to make sure you aren't using that pain as a prop in some role you have developed for yourself.

Sometimes, especially when money is involved, people in positions of authority may encourage you to maintain your dependence on your pain. If you are involved in litigation over a back injury, this may be done inadvertently, in the normal course of preparing your case. Your lawyer will call you up from time to time and ask, "How's your back?" You may not have thought about your back for weeks, but now he has made you focus on it. Since you are going to court over it, you are not about to embarrass him or yourself by getting well too soon. The last thing you're likely to say is, "Drop the case — my back is all better." Yet, medically speaking, that might be the smartest thing you could say.

A lawyer may also encourage you to prolong your pain as a cautionary measure: "We don't want to settle until you're completely well. Now, when was the last time you were ever completely well, with not so much as a twinge of pain or a stiff joint anywhere?" Advice like that may be smart law but it's bad medicine.

Compensation boards and accident-insurance schemes can be even more blatant about encouraging you to cultivate your back pain. That's not what they intend to do, but occasionally the system seems to operate that way. Instead of motivating you to recover and return to work, the system rewards you for feeling pain and punishes you for getting well.

If you have ever filed a claim for compensation or accident insurance, you will probably identify readily with the man in this next story, even if your job and personal circumstances are different from his. This man is a poorly educated immigrant who digs ditches for a living. He is hard at work one summer morning when he wrenches his back. Quite properly, he quits working and claims compensation from a government-operated fund and accident insurance from a scheme run by his employer.

His sore back keeps him off the job for six months, and the payments he receives make it possible for him to visit his sunny native land. He spends four months there, visiting with old friends and relatives.

Shortly before Christmas he returns home feeling much better and decides to go back to work in the new year. On the second day of January he pulls himself out of bed at 6 a.m. and rejoins his work crew. It's still dark outside. The weather is cold and snowy. The ground is frozen. The moment he puts shovel to earth, his back pain hits him again. Maybe you can think of several reasons why he should keep right on working, but at this moment he can't think of any. On the contrary, he can find at least four reasons why he'd be far better off if he went back on the sick list:

1. After four months of vacationing in the sunshine, who needs cold winds, snow, and frozen ground? And the man is not malingering. He's reacting normally. How great do you feel on the first day after your vacation, when you have to pry yourself out of bed and get back to work? Try getting back into harness after six months of nothing to do.

2. His back is sore again. And no wonder. Six months' idleness has left his physique in bad shape, and yet he feels he must prove that he's as good a ditch-digger as ever. Nobody has shown him there are ways of digging that will protect his back against unnecessary strain. What's worse, this is the first back pain he's felt in three months.

3. He's convinced that with every bit of pain he feels, he is causing permanent new damage to his back.

Nobody has told him what's wrong with his spine. It's only a simple case of facet pain, aggravated by the strain of digging, but he doesn't know that hurting is not the same as harming.

4. Financially speaking, he's crazy to be working again when he could be collecting benefits. Since his workers' compensation and his insurance benefits are both tax free, he was pocketing as much money while he was idle as he normally takes home in wages, after taxes, for mucking around in a half-frozen ditch.

Put yourself in his place. What would you do in those circumstances?

Your answer will depend on what you want out of life. I've thought a lot about that question, and I think that if I felt the way that ditch-digger feels — and if I had as many misconceptions as he has about back pain — I'd probably walk right off the job and go back on compensation.

The only trouble with my decision is that I would be stuck with the back pain. If it got better, I'd have to go back to work, and the whole cycle would start over again. But how long could I nurture my back pain? And what would I do when back pain had become my sole occupation and the compensation benefits had run out? I couldn't afford to be in pain for nothing, but I would be forced to do that — or go back to work.

I can't predict what your decision would be in those circumstances. But one basic purpose of this book is to point out the temptations and pitfalls of becoming a "professional" victim of back pain. I assume that you must be serious about ridding yourself of your pain and discovering ways of leading a normal life.

If that's truly your goal, you must make yourself aware of the part that tension, focus, and body language may be playing in your responses to back pain.

You must acquire factual knowledge about the mechanics of your back trouble, so that you can dispel your fears and no longer allow physical pain to trigger destructive emotional responses.

And you must resolve never to succumb to any person or any situation that may tempt you to prolong your pain.

7 Can a Chiropractor Help?

Sooner or later, many people with low-back pain give up on their doctors and turn elsewhere for help.

Typically, they will visit chiropractors or other practitioners whose theories and techniques lie somewhere on the fringes of conventional medicine. Some patients, perhaps those who are well-to-do but even some who are not, may be inclined to travel to a distant spot on the globe for treatments at expensive clinics or spas. Whatever treatment they choose, a few people come away feeling better than they have in years. But others end up more discouraged than ever, after suffering continuing pain, disappointment, and expense.

Anyone who is disenchanted with conventional doctors will have no trouble finding promising alternatives — chiropractors, homeopaths, herbalists, osteopaths, and various others. Osteopaths may resent being included in this group, since they enjoy the status of doctors in several parts of the world, including the United States. Nevertheless, osteopathy does represent an alternative to conventional medicine, and my own impression, from what I have read and know of their work, is that osteopaths place a much greater value on manipulative therapy than I believe is justified.

Recently the most faddish alternative in the treatment of back pain has been acupuncture. I find it a disturbing phenomenon because it strikes me as a novel and unproven treatment that raises false hopes among thousands, perhaps millions, of backache vic-

Either way, you'd have an inadequate notion of what a playing card looks like. The same limitations are faced by any practitioner trying to rely on a single X-ray.

Often, for reasons that have no foundation in medical knowledge, the chiropractor's X-ray may include your head, even though it is your back he is trying to diagnose. That's not dangerous, but it's pointless. Meanwhile, that single X-ray may omit a detailed view of your low back, where the trouble is usually found.

Even when they are shot thoroughly and properly, X-rays have serious limitations as a diagnostic tool. Yet chiropractors rely on X-rays extensively. Apparently some of them do not realize that the physical changes seen on the X-ray plate will not necessarily be the ones responsible for the pain you are feeling at the time. Doctors have an old expression: you can't X-ray pain. The wear and tear that is causing you pain today may remain undetectable by X-ray for years. Or you may even have a painful condition that never shows up on an X-ray plate. Discs, for example, do not appear on X-rays. You can have a painfully protruding disc and still take an X-ray that looks perfectly normal.

Being aware of the simplistic faith that many chiropractors have in X-rays, I was amused not long ago to see a chiropractor pop up on television one evening, demonstrating his use of X-rays. He was working on a male patient's back, with an X-ray film conspicuously displayed on the wall near by. As he simulated his treatment of the patient's spinal column, the chiropractor's eyes darted back and forth repeatedly between patient and X-ray. He gave the impression that he was closely relating the X-ray information to his manipulation of the patient's spine. What wasn't made clear was that only one of the many structures visible on that X-ray could be felt on the patient's back. In other words, there was really nothing to relate. Even the general position of the vertebrae can be determined with more certainty by touch alone. Did

you ever drive through a busy intersection in a strang
city and try to read a street map at the same time?
you don't know where you're going by then, it's too lat
to look. What the television audience saw going on i
front of the camera that evening may have been goo
show business, but it was hokey medicine.

Whether they actually say so or not, many chiro
practors give the impression that they can somehow
place their hands on a person's spine and shift mis
placed bones back into position. Anyone who harbor
that concept has no realistic idea of the anatomy of th
human back. A chiropractor who holds that view ha
probably never actually touched a living spine in hi
life. He works on every patient's back entirely fror
outside the body. I suspect that such a chiropractor'
ideas about the interior of the human back are base
on the study of skeletons conveniently stripped o
their muscles, ligaments, fat, and skin. When yo
study the backbone that way, you gain no apprecia
tion of the way a spine would resist manipulation.

While I agree that manipulation has its place in bacl
treatment — for instance, in the relief of muscl
spasms, or in the freeing up of stiff joints — th
proponents of manipulation overstate its value.
think they do this often out of ignorance. Let me tel
you about an experience I had with a person who is —
or should be — as knowledgeable about the humar
back as any chiropractor. This person is a physiothera
pist, an accepted member of the medical community

This man — let's call him Jack Johnson — found tha
family doctors in his community were referring quite ¡
number of back patients to him. For this reason, h
wanted to pick up any additional skill or knowledge h
could acquire on the subject of back pain. He came t
me, asking for advice. I decided it would be useful fo
him to observe the spinal operation I was about tc
perform on a young woman suffering from a seques
trated disc.

Now, Jack Johnson was a man with better qualifications than the average physiotherapist. I judged him to be a person of considerable intelligence, and his credentials showed that he had trained in a first-class institution in Europe. He was a firm believer in the concept of spinal manipulation. Apparently he had accepted the idea that spines can be "adjusted" readily by movement and massage. Yet the operation he observed that day was the first back surgery he had ever seen. In other words, he had never before set eyes on the backbone of a living human being.

I made the incision. My twenty-six-year-old patient was a woman you might describe as chubby but certainly not obese. Cutting through the skin, I came first to a layer of fat about an inch thick. Beneath that, a layer of muscle — another inch. Next, we encountered a second layer of muscle on the back of the spinal joints, and we stripped away a small portion of that muscle to expose the bone.

With the rearmost part of the backbone in view, we could see the roofs of those little "Monopoly houses" with the spines of the vertebrae projecting upwards like tiny chimneys. We were two inches, at least, beneath the surface of the patient's skin. I exposed enough of the spine that I was able to grasp two of the spiny projections with surgical instruments. To make a point to my observing friend, I took hold of the bones and tried to move them back and forth. They budged less than a quarter of an inch. There was no way I could "manipulate" them, even while grasping those two adjacent bones with heavy forceps. I couldn't do what that physiotherapist always thought he had been doing while working on a patient's back from the outside.

Another point had become obvious: manipulation could not be the precise art its proponents claimed it to be. The joints in the patient's back were two inches from the surface, were identified only by slight bulges along the edge of the bony "roof," and were only half an inch apart. To appreciate what I'm saying here, lay two parallel rows of pennies, two dozen in each row, on top of a table and cover them with a two-inch thickness of newspaper. Now see if you can locate the third penny from the end on the left. Impossible, isn't it? Yet that's what a proponent of manipulation is claiming to do, in effect, when he purports to manipulate, say, your left facet joint at the L_5 level.

Carrying on with the surgery, I penetrated the bony back of the spinal canal, worked through the cavity beyond it, and came to the disc, where I plucked out the loose fragment of disc that had been causing her pain.

By now, Jack Johnson had another point to ponder: the impossibility of the so-called disc adjustment. He realized that while it's difficult enough to manipulate individual spinal joints by laying hands on the surface of the skin, it's preposterous to believe that a bulging disc can be "adjusted" by exerting direct pressure on the back. He had to ask himself how anyone's spinal discs might be affected by manual contact through that multiple barrier of skin, fat, muscle, bone, and spinal canal. The answer, of course, is that there is no way.

Put your two rows of pennies into a desk drawer, shut the drawer, and see how well you can feel them through the top of the desk. That's what a "manipulator" is doing when he feels your back and declares, "I can feel your disc is out of place."

I doubt whether one chiropractor in a hundred has seen half as much as Jack Johnson saw in that one operation. Yet many chiropractors speak glibly of realigning your L_5 joint or slipping your L_{3-4} disc back into place, as though your interior body parts could be shifted around as readily as pawns on a chessboard.

Chiropractic treatment is not useless. Like any other form of skilled manipulation, it can put your spine through a useful range of movements, just as a series of bending and stretching exercises would in a somewhat different way. And it is a medical fact that manipulation sometimes relieves muscle spasms, thereby reducing or eliminating pain.

And manipulation can shorten the duration of an acute attack. In other words, chiropractic has its uses for people who need what the chiropractor has to offer: the relief of some forms of acute paraspinal muscle spasm through manipulation of the neck or low back.

Certainly chiropractors go too far when they suggest that manipulation will prevent muscle spasms as well as cure them. A muscle spasm is an extreme form of tension, a tightening that occurs under physical or emotional stress. That tightness may be loosened by manipulation, but no amount of manipulation carried out at a given moment can prevent a spasm from happening later. The same is true of "maintaining spinal alignment" through chiropractic "adjustments." The discs of your spine do not slip, and the facet joints do not keep "jumping out." Everything is already in place — there is nothing to "put back." And manipulation can do nothing to prevent the natural wear that is the source of common backache. Chiropractors who suggest otherwise are either trading on the popular mystique of the back or merely revealing their own ignorance of the way the back works.

In some circumstances, then, manipulation is useful, notably in the relief of muscle spasms. In other cases it is useless but probably harmless, as in so-called "preventive" therapy. In certain other instances, it can be risky; if a patient has a disc pressing on a nerve, for example, manipulation could seriously aggravate the pressure and the pain.

I never hesitate to recommend manipulative therapy for my patients if I believe it will be safe and useful. But I usually refer such cases to physiotherapists. A good physiotherapist can manipulate a patient's body

just as ably and effectively as any chiropractor —
and will do so, I might add, without the doubletalk
about spines being out of line or one leg being longer
than the other. I know I can count on the physiotherapist to keep in touch with me throughout the period of
treatment in the interest of the patient, whose progress
becomes our common concern. Most chiropractors, on
the other hand, are not team players — at least not
with doctors. My patient would become the chiropractor's patient, and I would be expected to have nothing
further to say about the treatment. That's not my idea
of the best way to help people get well.

I am optimistic, however, that there will be more co-
operation in the future between chiropractors and
physicians. Young chiropractors seem more inclined
than their elders to distinguish between back patients
who can benefit from manipulation and those who
need surgery instead. No longer is the entire profession devoted to selling chiropractic as the magic cure-
all. Referrals from chiropractors to doctors are becoming more frequent — a healthy sign, in my view.

By now you may be wondering, "If the benefits of
chiropractic are as limited as he says, why are chiropractors flourishing? And why do we keep hearing
enthusiastic stories from people who say their chiropractors helped them after their own doctors failed?"

The answer is that chiropractors enjoy a degree of
popularity and credit far out of proportion to the
medical value of their art. On the basis of my own
experience and discussions with thousands of back
patients who have been to chiropractors, I believe you
have roughly a fifty-fifty chance of relieving your
back pain by seeing a chiropractor. That estimate,
however, may make manipulation sound more effective than it is. Other factors help the chiropractor look
good, especially if you go to him after a disenchanting
experience with a doctor.

Here are the factors that most often work to the
chiropractor's advantage.

The Last-Resort Syndrome

When your doctor fails to solve your back problem, you wonder, "Is he not a very good doctor, or am I a hopeless case? Whichever it is, what have I got to lose by trying a chiropractor?"

Well, you haven't much to lose. But once you're in that state of mind, your chiropractor can hardly lose, either. After he has treated you, your back will feel better or it won't. If it feels better, the chiropractor wins full marks. He has succeeded where your doctor failed. You tell all your friends about him. If your back doesn't feel better, that's hardly the chiropractor's fault. After all, your doctor — a fully qualified MD — couldn't cure it either. But you don't tell your friends that you saw a doctor and a chiropractor, both of whom were no good. You tell them you have a back problem that has baffled at least two medical specialists.

Salesmanship

Let's pretend you inherited some money and are trying to choose between two investment dealers.

Mr. A tells you: "I suppose we might, uh, find some suitable stock or bond for you, but the market is, uh, rather uncertain at the best of times. Of course, I would be willing to look into it and do whatever I could, but I must warn you that I couldn't guarantee . . ."

Mr. B tells you: "Look — I've made a lot of people wealthy in the past five years. Seven of my clients had to borrow bus fare to get here. Today they're millionaires. I can do the same for you. Now this is my plan. . . ."

Would you believe me if I told you Mr. A knows more about investing than Mr. B does? You wouldn't want to believe it, would you?

People with back problems have the same kind of

trouble maintaining confidence in a doctor who sounds like the medical equivalent of Mr. A. And too many doctors do. They hem and haw and neglect to communicate even half of what they know about the patient's condition or what can be done about it. There is nothing wrong with being thoughtful and cautious, especially in medicine, but it is self-defeating to be so non-committal that people doubt the doctor's professional abilities.

Chiropractors don't make that mistake. When you walk into a chiropractor's office, he greets you warmly, examines you with expert aplomb, and announces: "No wonder you're having pain. Your problem is a C_{5-6} subluxation that needs to be adjusted four millimeters to the left. If you'd like to recline here on this table, I can look after it for you right now."

Harsher critics than I have suggested that in the art of manipulation, some chiropractors are even more adept with people than with spines.

The Equality Hangup

I can explain this phenomenon by describing the experience of a colleague while he was shepherding six medical students through rounds in a hospital. In the emergency ward they came upon a woman with acute appendicitis. My friend knew what was wrong with her, but by way of teaching the art of diagnosis, he withheld that knowledge and asked each student, in turn, to examine her and give an opinion.

The first student said the patient needed her gall bladder removed. The next said she had a bowel problem. The third thought it was a stomach ulcer. And so on. Six students offered six different diagnoses — all of them wrong. Finally, my colleague enlightened them. "This woman," he announced, "has acute appendicitis. In fact, it is so acute that we are taking her to the operating room within the hour."

At that moment, the patient spoke up.

"Wait a minute!" she told the doctor. "You're only one out of seven. If you guys can't agree on what's wrong with me, nobody is taking out my appendix!"

If you are a back patient who has been examined by, perhaps, four doctors who provided four different — or different-sounding — diagnoses, I can't blame you if you think the whole thing is just a guessing game, with one man's opinion as good as another's. If that were so, diagnosticians wouldn't need to spend time acquiring training and experience. They could diagnose you by taking a public-opinion poll out on the street. But some people favor this notion of equality among experts, as though there were no degrees of experience or expertise. That is a dangerous attitude to carry with you into the office of any practitioner — doctor or chiropractor.

The Remission Factor

Sore backs have good days and bad days. If you were a person without conscience, you could use that fact to make a lot of money. You could set up a shop where you offered to make anyone's back feel better by treating it with a magic blue light. It would be just an ordinary light, of course, but your customers wouldn't know that. You'd persuade them to pay you $100 for a series of treatments, and you would know that out of every ten customers, at least one would probably be "cured" during the period of treatment, because it would always be somebody's turn to have his back get better all by itself.

You would know, too, that anyone who felt better after your treatments would tell everybody he met, thereby providing you with free advertising — and a good reputation you didn't deserve. Your disappointed customers wouldn't say much to anyone; they'd feel too sheepish at having been taken.

The Placebo Effect

This is a factor that works to the advantage of every practitioner at some time, and chiropractors can hardly be criticized for enjoying its benefits. But it does account partly for the credit they receive as healers. A placebo, as you probably know, is a harmless "medicine" with no medicinal value. It relieves some people of pain through the power of suggestion. Suppose you line up a hundred people, all of whom have the same chronic back pain. You give each of them a sugar pill and tell them it will relieve their pain. Statistics show that if you are convincing, about thirty of those people will feel better. Of course, you haven't done a thing to correct the cause of their pain; but temporarily, at least, they are "cured."

A placebo does not have to be a pill. The laying on of hands can achieve the same result. Any treatment in which the practitioner touches the patient's body — such as manipulation of the spine — carries with it a powerful Placebo Effect.

Some of the most recent studies of the Placebo Effect suggest that this phenomenon may occur through the spontaneous release of endorphins, those natural opiates that are credited with the pain-relieving effect of acupuncture. If this is so, the Placebo Effect is a matter of tricking a person's body into relieving pain by means of the body's own chemistry. In other words, one person out of every three, far from being the gullible "victim" of the placebo, is fortunate in unconsciously possessing the power to release body chemicals that kill pain. Which brings up an intriguing question: can the other two-thirds of the population be trained or induced to make use of this same power?

In simpler times, long before anyone had heard of endorphins, the Placebo Effect was exploited with stunning commercial success. Just one example is the Toronto doctor who, years ago, collected a huge following by having his arthritis patients listen to a particular radio station at specified times of the day. At those times, he assured them, he was beaming soundless "healing waves" that would cure arthritis. The patient merely had to hold the affected part close to the radio speaker and — the doctor never had to say it — believe. As far as I know, the results were not recorded methodically, but it seems likely that at least a few of the faithful experienced some relief from arthritic pain.

When a new patient comes to me with acute back pain, I examine him or her and then I usually prescribe several days' rest. Almost invariably the patient asks, "But aren't you going to do anything?"

And all I can say is, "But I am doing something — I'm telling you to go home and rest."

That's the best prescription I can offer such a person at that moment, but it doesn't involve pills, drugs, manipulation, heat treatment, or the laying on of healing hands. Consequently, if I want the Placebo Effect to work for me, I must be completely convincing in my assurance that rest alone will work, and I must be quite precise in my instructions regarding rest, so that the patient feels that something effective is under way.

The Pilgrim Syndrome

The factors that work in favor of chiropractors also enhance the popularity and reputations of health spas and clinics that specialize in treating sore backs. The operators of such establishments usually manage, as well, to take advantage of what I call the Pilgrim Syndrome. This syndrome begins in the minds of the people who say, "I don't care how much it costs — I want the best!" It may not surprise you to learn that there are doctors who are willing to cater to such wishes.

The "clinic," as its patients often come to call it, is

usually located in a fairly inaccessible, if not foreign, setting. If you're off to see The Wizard, you want to look him up in Oz, not Cleveland. The clinic usually has a waiting list, implying an exclusive and selected clientele. Its principal doctors, who are often its administrators as well, have impressive qualifications which appear to be — and probably are — recognized by the medical establishment. At the same time, these doctors make it clear that they are, by their own choosing, and by reason of their special skills and concerns, practitioners who stand apart from the main body of the profession.

The clinic's literature is clearly intended to be seductively persuasive. It is long on emotion and salesmanship and short on hard facts and medical details. Results are never described in clinical terms — only in rave notices. One establishment in California, for instance, promotes itself with a magazine-style booklet containing an article describing how its "eager and zealous" patients acquire a "new awareness of well-being, joy of living and self-renewal." The article even claims success with the "hopelessly diseased" — a feat I first thought impossible, by definition. Then I came upon a second article in which one of the "hopeless cases," a housewife and mother just out of her twenties, explained the secret: "miracles."

The crucial moment in her personal saga was an encounter with her visiting family, the sort of situation from which great soap opera is made:

I'll never forget the first day I walked without the aid of my cane. My family unexpectedly decided to join me for supper. They rushed past me in the corridor, eager to catch me in the dining room. As they passed by me, I recognized them and called out to them. They turned and stared in open-mouthed wonder, and as the wonder turned to joy, we three embraced and tears of happiness

streamed down our faces. We knew we could
make it: Mommy was getting well!

Unfortunately for the curious reader, Mommy never
does get around to describing what was wrong with
her back or how the clinic helped her. Such details are
perhaps not considered important to the readers of the
clinic's promotional literature. But money is. The
booklet tells how another patient, also a woman,
"successfully rehabilitated" in only sixty-three days
after four years in bed with a bad back, ran up a bill of
$38,000. The clinic didn't get all of that amount; part of
it was for "prior expense" and part for "related
settlements" (whatever those two items mean), and
the rest (amount unspecified) was for "our program
charge."

Far from seeing this sum as exorbitant — and who
can say she didn't get full value for the money? — the
administrators of the clinic calculate that without
their treatment the woman's medical insurance company would have paid out $328,000 "to support this
lady's anticipated lifetime need for drugs, medical
care, food, shelter and clothing." By a process of
unassailable mathematics, they calculate that the
woman's $38,000 bill thus represented a saving to the
insurance company of a tidy $290,000. In fact, in
treating sixty patients annually and saving them an
average of $200,000 apiece, this California clinic
estimates that it is saving patients or their insurance
companies $12,000,000 a year.

Any doctor, especially a back doctor, may encounter
the Pilgrim Syndrome without having encouraged it.
This has happened to me, even though I have not yet
issued bulletins on how many millions I am saving the
insurance industry every year. My most memorable
pilgrim was a middle-aged woman — from California,
ironically — who had decided that a trek to Toronto
would be her salvation. She was in such bad shape

that she needed an ambulance to take her to the hospital from the airport. I soon realized that her mild, Type Two back pain was not the real problem. She had developed a complete life-style built around her back pain, with which she ruled her family and dominated her husband. Throughout her stay in a Toronto hospital, our medical team administered copious amounts of psychology, psychiatry, physical therapy, and sympathetic listening.

In three weeks she was up and about and ready to go home. As she walked happily out of the hospital, without the use of her cane, she couldn't find words glowing enough to express her gratitude. Apparently this woman has experienced the same sort of "awareness of well-being" and "self-renewal" advertised by that clinic in her home state — but at one-tenth the cost. Rather than the $38,000 incurred by the woman who had been "successfully rehabilitated" in sixty-three days, our patient managed her twenty-one-day recovery for something less than $4,000, including hospital bed and air fare.

The moral of this story? Buyer beware. But beyond that maxim, remember that dependence on less conventional or "alternative" medicine is simply unnecessary. The power to control and relieve your back pain, as you will discover, lies with you.

8 Step into My Examining Room

I hope some readers of this book will find that they can apply my advice with such rewarding results that they will never have to see a doctor about their backs.

There are bound to be many more, however, who for various reasons will have their back problems diagnosed professionally. In case you become one of them, you ought to have some idea of what to expect. You will be doing both your doctor and yourself a favor if you go prepared to answer his questions and undergo an examination without any qualms about the things he will do to you.

Every doctor has his own style and favorite techniques, but the description here of my procedure is fairly typical of what you can expect when you see your own doctor.

If you come to me complaining of pain in your lower back, I begin with a series of questions about your medical history and personal habits. Often, this proves to be the most important and useful stage of a patient's examination. I want to know everything you can tell me about your pain, and everything about yourself that could be relevant to your back problem. When did the pain first occur? What was it like then? Has it changed? Has it spread? Does it hamper your normal activities? If so, which ones and how? Does it upset you? And so forth.

I also ask about your general health and personal background: past illnesses; surgery, if any; patterns of illness in your family; details about your job, your work habits, your recreational pursuits, your life-style.

You will be helping us both if you answer my questions not just frankly but precisely too. It's not enough, for instance, merely to say that you have pain in your legs. I want to know exactly where — only in your thigh or right down into your toes? And is there numbness or tingling, or a sensation of burning or cold?

Let's assume now that you are not in acute pain and that I can go ahead with a complete physical examination of your back. I ask you to strip down to your underwear and slip into an examining gown that opens at the back. The examination will consist of a standard sequence of observations and tests, to be done while you are standing, sitting, kneeling, bending, and lying in various positions. The whole examination will take no more than five minutes.

If you tried the self-diagnosis set out in Chapter Four, you will recognize many of the tests I describe here. To begin, I ask you to stand up and show me whether you can bend your upper body backwards and forwards without causing additional pain. This provides significant clues as to whether your problem might be Type One, a worn facet joint, which is painful on bending back; or Type Two, a protruding disc, which is painful on bending forward.

Next, while you are still standing, I ask you to see how well you can rise up on your toes, ten times on both feet at once, then ten times, in turn, on each foot separately. Here, I am looking for any sign that Type Three back trouble, a pinched nerve, might have made one calf weaker than the other.

I ask you next to kneel on a chair while I test your ankle reflexes by tapping your Achilles' tendons. Differences in your reflexes from one ankle to another will also suggest the possibility of a damaged nerve.

Now I ask you to turn around and sit on the chair with your feet flat on the floor. Squatting in front of you, I press down firmly with my hand against the top of each foot in turn, asking you to see how well you can lift the forefoot against my downward pressure. Again, I'm looking for clues to Type Three pain.

Incidentally, this is a test where it is impossible to fake weakness. I'm not suggesting that you have come into my office pretending to have back pain that isn't there; very few people do that. But quite a number of patients are fearful that certain limitations are so faint or subtle that they will be overlooked during the examination. And so they exaggerate these conditions, to make sure the doctor will take due note of them. Let me advise you against this inclination, because it can backfire. A doctor who realizes you are exaggerating your condition may decide that you are a complete fake. If that happens, he may ignore genuine signs of trouble.

In any case, you can't deceive me with the foot-raising exercise I just described. What I am looking for in this test is muscular weakness. If your foot is truly weak, it will sink to the floor smoothly under my downward pressure. If it is normal, you will find it impossible to simulate that smooth downward motion. Either you have to let go suddenly, or else allow your foot to descend in a series of little "cogwheel" steps, which any competent examiner will detect. In fact, a good back examination is designed to cross-check certain findings. People who are malingering may be able to fake one test but they will be caught out by another that should match but doesn't.

To return to the examination, next I have you stand beside the examining table, bending forward to rest your forearms on the table. Now I palpate (feel) your spinal column with my fingers and palms. Even though I am gentle, you may find it necessary to let me know, in words, or with gasps or flinches, whenever I come to a tender spot on your spine. Those tender places, by the way, are not necessarily the prime sources of your pain. It is altogether likely that they are points of "referred" pain — that is, pain radiated from some other location. For this reason, the object of palpating your spine is not only to find the tender spots but also to pick up other clues, such as lumps caused by inflammation, or a slight spinal curvature.

In your next position you are seated on the edge of the examining table as I test your knee reflexes. Here I am not looking for good or poor reflexes but for differences between one leg and the other.

Now it's time for you to lie on the table, face up, as I test your hips — first by having you draw your knees up to your chest, then by turning your feet gently outward, to rotate your hip joints. If either test causes pain, I'll look further for hip problems.

Chances are we'll be able to go on to the next tests, those for an irritated nerve. While you remain face up on the table, I lift your leg with the knee held straight to see whether this causes pain to run from your back down your leg. Next, I press behind your knee at the point where the sciatic nerve passes close to the bone. If the nerve is inflamed, the pressure of my thumb will cause pain up or down your leg.

I also check for normal nerve function by pricking your legs and feet with a pin, and testing power in muscles I haven't tested so far.

Now I check to see whether your back pain might be originating from some other part of your body, by gently pressing on your kidneys and abdomen and by checking the pulses in your legs.

I make sure you are not suffering from damage to your spinal cord by stroking the soles of your feet with the pointed handle of my reflex hammer. If your spinal cord is free of problems your reflexes will make your toes curl.

If my findings so far suggest Type Three trouble, I will ask you to lie first on one side and then on the other while I do some additional tests of your leg muscle power.

In the last position of my examination sequence, you

are lying face down on the table as I lift your legs backwards one at a time. If the nerve that runs from your back into the front of your leg is irritated from your back trouble, you will feel pain in the front of your thigh.

Using the pinprick technique again, I test sensation in the upper area of your buttocks. A complete loss of sensation here indicates serious nerve damage. This finding, if combined with an abnormality that would be revealed during the rectal examination that follows, would prompt me to immediate action. This is a very serious condition — a rare variation of Type Three trouble — that may require emergency surgery. It is the only exception to the general rule that low-back trouble can be treated with bed rest, followed by a period in which your doctor has time to wait and see whether your back gets better by itself. This is such a rare condition that in the course of examining several thousand back patients a year over the past decade or more, I have seen only five or six of these cases.

Next I test the power of your buttock muscles — by pressing on your buttocks while you tense them. Weakness on one side or the other is an indication that you might have Type Three back trouble. This is another test where it's difficult for a patient to fake the results. That means it's useful in helping me decide whether a patient is exaggerating his symptoms. It is very difficult to tighten just one of your buttocks at a time, as you can discover for yourself.

Depending on what I've found so far, I may do a rectal examination. If you are a man, this examination includes feeling the prostate gland, which is one location that is always checked for the possibility of cancer. In both men and women I check the muscle "tone" or resiliency and the constriction reflex of your anal sphincter. If they were not normal I would suspect that you had a protruding disc exerting pressure on several nerves inside the spinal canal, a condition known as central disc herniation. This finding would be the follow-up I anticipated earlier when I found that you had lost all sensation in your upper buttocks, as demonstrated in the pinprick test. As I have already stressed, this is a rare and serious condition, and I bring it up again only because it explains one good reason for a rectal examination, which otherwise may not be necessary in the course of a standard examination of your back.

That would complete your first visit, and chances are I would diagnose your problem as one of the three types of common back pain.

At this point you may be wondering why I haven't ordered X-rays, blood samples, or other tests.

Well, I could do so, of course, but they would have no more value in a case of common back pain than finding out whether you respond to simple treatment — bed rest during acute attacks of pain, then abdominal exercises and the adoption of good postural habits. Whether you are just recovering from an acute attack or suffering from chronic backache, I want to see whether you improve with this conservative treatment over a period of, say, two months.

If you haven't improved by then, there would still be plenty of time to explore the possibility of some other cause, such as disease or congenital abnormality. You might consider this a rather casual attitude on my part, but it's not. The rarer causes that attack suddenly and develop quickly, such as central disc herniation, always include telltale symptoms that I would detect on your first visit. The rare conditions that can't be detected so readily take months to develop. A few weeks' delay would make no difference to your chances of recovery.

The likeliest outcome of that conservative treatment is that your back will show marked improvement. I have found that one-third of the patients with chronic backache who return to me in two months are better. Another one-third of them are showing enough improvement that we know the treatment is working well; their recovery will just take a little longer. The other third show no improvement. By questioning this group, however, I have discovered that two out of three of these people have failed to improve because they have ignored the routine I set out for them.

That leaves only about ten percent of my chronic patients with unexplained backache. These are the people who should have some additional diagnostic work done, in case their back pain is not the result of normal wear and tear, or in the event that we need to prepare for surgery.

Now that you realize that the great majority of people who come to me are helped by simple, conservative treatment, I'm sure you can see why I don't believe in spending time and money on X-rays or tests for every patient who walks into my office.

Mind you, there are many excellent doctors who take X-rays during a first visit. If your doctor includes X-rays along with questions about your medical history and an examination of your back, you shouldn't conclude that he isn't good at his job. All I would say is that he and I happen to differ on this point of procedure.

Generally speaking, the X-rays and other additional tests used in diagnosing back problems can accomplish only two basic things:

1. They can help pinpoint the location of trouble by showing where abnormal conditions exist.
2. They can help rule out generalized disease by showing that the patient does not have the specific conditions which such a disease would cause.

Pinpointing the exact location of, say, a worn facet joint is a wasteful exercise for anyone who is going to treat his whole back simply with rest and exercise. It could hardly matter less to him whether his trouble is at the L_4 or the L_5 level.

And as for the function of ruling out disease or congenital abnormalities, proper conservative care and treatment will accomplish that too — without the risk, pain, expense, or expenditure of professional time that some medical tests may entail.

Please do not misunderstand what I am saying here. I am not implying for a moment that I consider diagnostic tests unnecessary or valueless; far from it. In fact I use them frequently. All I am saying is that most patients can do without them because their backs get better rapidly enough that further investigation is unnecessary.

In case you are a back patient who requires X-ray or additional testing, let me offer you a brief description and a personal opinion of each test.

Plain X-Rays

These are the X-rays we have all had at some time — at the dentist's or during routine checks for chest disease. The X-ray is a useful tool, but it has severe limitations. Many patients, I know, think of the X-ray as a sort of medical photograph. I only wish it were that good. If I take an X-ray of your back, the film does not show a photo of your spine; it shows just a shadow cast by the bones of your spine and by the other parts of your body as the rays pass through — or fail to pass through — these structures.

Furthermore, an X-ray is a photographic negative. This means that the more it is exposed to light, the darker the film becomes. This can be confusing in itself, as you will recall from what you saw the last time you looked at the negative of a favorite snapshot. The bones of your spine absorb the X-ray beam and therefore appear white on the X-ray plate. The other parts, such as muscles and internal organs, allow much of the beam to pass through, producing darker areas on the film. Reading an X-ray is like trying to "read" the intricate pattern on a painted lampshade by looking only at the shadows it casts on a nearby wall — and doing the whole thing in reverse. A single

X-ray of your spine can't reveal nearly enough. Views from several angles or at several depths are necessary.

While an X-ray shows bone and dense muscle, other tissue appears only faintly. It doesn't show nerves or discs, except as dark spaces beside the whiteness of bone, and their shapes are implied rather than visible. An X-ray will show neither a physical change in a muscle nor a muscle spasm. And of course it cannot show pain.

It will show a fracture. It can show an advanced case of wear and tear. It can show the little bony projections we call bone spurs or, more properly, osteophytes. It will show a case of scoliosis, which is abnormal curvature of the spine. It will show a vertebra that has slipped (spondylolisthesis) or a vertebra with a defect in it (spondylolysis) or an alteration that has taken place in the normal segmentation of the lumbar and sacral regions.

I remember hearing my father say he had an extra bone in his back. When I saw his X-rays I realized that what he had is technically called lumbarization. Translated from Doctor, it means that one of the five normally fused sacral vertebrae fails to join with the rest and is left as a movable bone in the lumbar region, separated from the sacrum by a fully formed disc. In effect, people with lumbarization have six lumbar vertebrae instead of the customary five, and only four sacral vertebrae instead of five. The total number of vertebrae in the spine is standard; they are just divided differently. Some people have the opposite variation — six sacral vertebrae and four lumbar vertebrae (sacralization). Some doctors suspect that these unusual forms of segmentation cause back pain, but this suspicion has never been confirmed.

An X-ray can show signs of soft-tissue trouble in the form of swelling. It can show certain patterns indicating such diseases as rheumatoid arthritis or ankylosing spondylitis. It would be unusual, however, to discover these by X-ray alone, since their symptoms should be obvious during a routine physical examination.

An X-ray can be much more useful if it has some basis of comparison. The X-ray you have taken next week will tell your doctor a lot more if he can compare it with the same view taken a few years earlier. That is one reason why it is not a good idea for anyone with back trouble to switch doctors without a referral. Sometimes when I ask new patients about old X-rays, they say, "My previous doctor has some, but I'd rather you didn't call him." When that happens, my hands are tied. It may take a little courage on your part to tell a doctor you're leaving him, but you won't be the first. In any medical practice, patients come and go. If you don't make that little exit speech so that your X-rays and records can be passed along, you are depriving your new doctor — and yourself — of an important advantage.

Blood Tests

From a small sample of your blood, a medical laboratory can tell me a lot about the health of your back.

A *hemoglobin test* will tell me about the condition of your bone marrow, where your red blood cells are made. If the marrow is abnormal, I may consider the possibility of several forms of cancer in your bones, including your spine.

A *count of white blood cells,* where normal, will help rule out the possibility that your body is harboring an infection.

A *sedimentation rate* — the speed with which your red blood cells settle in a glass tube — is an old-fashioned but useful test for ruling out the possibility of widespread disease as the cause of your back pain. Your doctor may use it if your back condition hasn't responded to rest and physical therapy.

Rheumatoid factor, also known as a latex fixation test, can be used to confirm that you do not have rheumatoid arthritis or some related condition. This test, however, is accurate only eighty-five percent of the time. In any case, no laboratory test, however accurate, can be expected to replace what a doctor learns from a patient's history and physical examination.

Blood calcium, phosphorus, and various enzymes. When rapid changes occur in the structure of the bone, calcium, phosphorus, and certain enzymes appear in the blood in increased amounts. They reflect the bones' reaction to several types of bone-forming or bone-destroying cancers and a variety of diseases that affect bone. Lab tests showing these chemicals to exist at normal levels will help rule out the possibility of cancer or generalized disease as a cause of back pain.

Urine Tests

Kidney infections sometimes produce low-back pain. Whenever the clinical picture indicates, I order a urine culture and routine urinalysis, to make sure the kidneys are not involved.

Electromyography and Nerve-Conduction Studies

Although these are two separate tests, they are often carried out together because they are done with the same machine.

Electromyography (EMG) is a means of studying the reaction of a muscle when it is stimulated by a nerve. A nerve-conduction study is an examination of a specific nerve's ability to conduct impulses.

Suppose, for example, that you have back pain and have lost the ability to lift your toes while your foot is flat on the floor. The culprit may be the muscle or the sciatic nerve or the nerve root that governs that foot action. The first possibility can be ruled out by the EMG, and the other two by a nerve-conduction study.

To conduct these tests, the examiner will insert

extremely fine needles at several points along the length of your leg. This test is uncomfortable but not painful. The needles are wired to an instrument that can show whether your muscular contractions and nerve impulses are normal. If they are, the doctor can conclude — by simple deduction — that the damage is located higher up, at the nerve root.

Bone Scanning

Certain changes in the bones of your spine can be located by injecting a harmless radioactive material called technetium into your bloodstream. Within a couple of hours the technetium settles into the bones. Its radiation, picked up by a device comparable to a Geiger counter, can be displayed on a screen and recorded as a "picture" similar to an X-ray. In a location where there is rapid bone growth, with the inclusion of a larger amount of technetium, such as in response to a bone-forming cancer, the picture will show a dense black area or "hot spot." This test is safe and painless and the technetium disappears rapidly.

Thermography

This test was devised to pinpoint trouble spots by detecting altered circulation. It is based on the theory that where there is inflammation there will be extra heat on the surface of the skin, created by an increased concentration of blood. Also, it is a fact that your nerves control the diameter of your blood vessels; therefore, if you have something wrong with a nerve, the size of the blood vessels may be altered and the flow of blood will be affected.

Personally, I am not enthusiastic about this test in the diagnosis of back pain. The variations in temperature are slight, and accurate measurements are difficult.

Ultrasound

Ultrasound is generating a great deal of enthusiasm among doctors in other specialties and for good reason. But as a tool for diagnosing back problems it is still in the experimental stage. It is a noble attempt to gather as much information as possible about your spine without invading your body in the process. A machine bounces high-frequency sound waves harmlessly off the structures in your back, and the resounding waves create a rather imprecise "picture" of your spine. X-rays are hard enough to interpret, but ultrasound results are even more difficult.

Tomography

A significant elaboration of the X-ray, tomography uses a machine that produces a whole series of "pictures," each taken at a slightly different depth in your body. Perhaps I can describe this process more clearly by using a child's birthday cake as an example of an X-ray subject. Suppose you made a traditional birthday cake and dropped several dozen coins into it at random. If you X-rayed the cake to locate the coins, you'd see only a confusing jumble of overlapping shapes, with no indication of whether a given coin was close to the surface or deep inside. A more reliable way of getting this information would be to cut a series of thin, parallel slices of cake, to see whether they contained any coins. Of course, we can't slice up your body or your spine that way, but the tomograph does that for us in pictures. It produces a dozen or so X-rays, each one a cut deeper than the last. Since we know the depth at which each cut was made, we can accurately identify the location of the objects we see in each picture. By studying the whole series of images, we can construct in our minds a composite picture of what your spine must look like.

Tomograms are harder to read than ordinary X-rays, but they reveal much more to the experienced eye. Like X-rays, however, they are limited to showing only the bones and other objects that block the passage of the X-ray beams.

The Myelogram

This delicate technique can help a surgeon pinpoint a disc problem before he operates. It uses an X-ray machine in conjunction with a colorless liquid that is radiopaque — that is, impervious to X-rays.

The test begins with the injection of the fluid into the patient's dural sac, which is the sheath surrounding the spinal cord and the nerve roots. The patient lies on a tilting table, and as X-rays are shot, he is tilted back and forth, so that the injected material flows slowly up and down his spine as it fills the space surrounding each nerve. The fluid appears white on the X-rays, while the indentations or outright obstructions from protruding discs show up as dark blotches. The myelogram does not show the discs. It outlines the defect a disc produces as it presses against the nerve sac. The disc remains invisible, even though opaque fluid is used.

A myelogram is not infallible. It may show an indentation from a bulging disc that is not in fact the cause of your pain. On the other hand, a disc may be sore without bulging enough to show up on the myelogram. Or a bulging disc may remain undetected on the myelogram because it is bulging in an area remote from the dural sac, where the test fluid lies.

The myelogram must be used with caution. Many people suffer headaches after a myelogram, but the discomfort usually disappears within twenty-four hours if the patient rests flat in bed. The headaches may last longer and will sometimes carry a suggestive effect that lasts indefinitely. Rightly or wrongly, some patients insist that their backs became worse after a myelogram. Even if that's not true, it's a problem for any patient who believes it.

In rare instances, the fluid creates an irritation of the inner lining of the dural sac. Such complications can be anticipated and avoided by a good myelographer. Even at that, I feel strongly that myelography should not be used as a routine diagnostic tool. Except in instances where the patient's condition defies diagnosis by less invasive forms of observation and testing, a myelogram should be avoided unless it is required in preparing for surgery. As a general rule, if you are not willing to have surgery, you should not have a myelogram.

The Discogram

This is another technique involving injection of a liquid opaque to X-rays. In this case, however, the material is injected directly into the disc, to see whether it is normal. In a normal disc, the injected fluid, unable to escape, shows on the X-ray as an almond-shaped blob inside the disc, centered between the two adjacent vertebrae. If the disc is ruptured or badly worn, the injected fluid quickly leaks out and disappears.

It's a painful test. No anesthetic is used, and the conclusions drawn depend partly on the character of the pain produced. Some doctors distrust this test because the disc that looks damaged may be painless, and some innocent-looking disc nearby may be causing the trouble.

The Epidural Venogram

This is one of two tests adopted in recent years as alternatives to injections into the discs or the dural space. In this test, radiopaque fluid is injected into veins in the groin and flows into the veins in the back. If a disc is bulging enough to compress a nerve root, it is usually bulging enough to compress a vein as well. In that case, the venogram may show an indentation into a vein, or, more likely, the obliteration of some blood vessels.

The results from an epidural venogram require a highly skilled interpreter. In experienced hands, however, this test becomes one of the most precise of all X-ray investigations. And for back patients it has the advantage of providing the least discomfort of almost any test involving an injection.

The Epiduragram

This test, in a sense, is the "opposite" of a myelogram: instead of being injected inside the dural sac, the radiopaque material is injected outside the sac and is allowed to flow all around the dura, to outline any bulging discs. Because the amount of fluid injected is greater than in the myelogram, and because it is allowed to travel over a wider area, many medical people feel it offers a better chance of detecting a disc protrusion. It has the added advantage of avoiding irritation to the inner lining of the sac, one of the recognized complications of myelography. This test has been used in Europe for over thirty years but has come into use in North America only much more recently.

Nerve-Root Injection

The purpose of this test is to determine which nerve root is to blame for an area of leg pain. A radiopaque liquid and a local anesthetic are mixed together and injected around the suspected root. The opaque fluid shows up on a fluoroscope, confirming that the correct nerve root has been injected. The anesthetic, of course, removes all feeling from that branch. If the pain ceases, the doctor knows he has located the trouble spot — *more or less.*

The problem is that adjacent nerve roots overlap in function. Instead of pinpointing the nerve root where the pain is originating, the test may throw suspicion on an "innocent" neighbor that is merely relaying the pain.

Facet Injection

Working on the same principle as the nerve-root injection and with the same mixture of fluids, this test helps determine which joint is to blame for facet pain. In my opinion, it's more accurate than nerve-root injection, although the same overlap can occur, raising the same question as to where the pain fibers actually originated. Even pinpointing the origin of the pain, however, doesn't solve the problem of what to do next. Unless the need for surgery is obvious — and it seldom is — conservative management may be the most sensible treatment. And in that case, it doesn't really matter which particular facet joint is causing the pain.

The CAT Scanner

Of all the clever techniques and ingenious devices used in diagnosing back problems, this one is the ultimate. In fact, if anyone asked me to name the single most impressive technological advance in medicine in the latter half of the twentieth century, I might pause two seconds before I said, "The CAT scanner." CAT stands for Computerized Axial Tomography. In other words, it's a fancy X-ray device. But calling it that is like saying Skylab was a complicated flying machine.

By comparison, the output of the CAT scanner makes tomography look like drawings on some caveman's wall. The tomograph produces its dozen or so serial X-rays of the bone structures of the back but leaves their interpretation entirely to a human expert. The

CAT scanner combines its own multiple exposures into a single "picture" with clarity and easy-to-read detail that I still find astounding whenever I see it.

The CAT scanner's strength lies partly in the way its computer can "read" the subtle differences it sees between one X-ray and the next — differences no human eye could ever detect. Having read these differences, the CAT scanner then accentuates them, all in proportion to their original intensity, so that they can be seen at a glance. In practical terms, this means that the CAT scanner, far from being limited to showing bony structures, can portray soft tissue. It can actually take pictures of the membranes surrounding the nerves; it can even show the internal structure of the spinal cord itself.

The CAT scanner's computer can also work by inference to "show" views that even it has never seen. For instance, it can show a side view that would be impossible to X-ray. It does this by taking many views of a frontal exposure, each at a slightly different depth. By detecting and "remembering" the subtle differences it has seen from one depth to the next, the CAT scanner can portray — by deductive memory — precisely what a side view must look like. By this means it enables doctors to see things inside a living human being that are denied them by any other methods.

Even as the ultimate diagnostic tool, however, the CAT scanner has limitations. Because of your spine's considerable length and its position in your body, curves and all, the CAT scanner, despite its remarkable flexibility, still can't capture some of the views that back doctors would like to see. At least not yet.

It's also an expensive machine — a million-dollar item costing perhaps another half a million dollars a year to operate. The cost factor generally limits CAT scanners to large hospitals in major cities and tends to restrict their use to cases that cannot be diagnosed by cheaper, less elaborate means.

But, personally, I can live with these drawbacks. For me, it's enough to know that when all else fails in a struggle with a particularly baffling diagnosis, I can turn to the CAT scanner as the ultimate weapon.

9 Poultices, Pulleys, and Phenylbutazone

Just as there is no scarcity of practitioners willing to treat your bad back, there is no shortage of backache remedies to choose from — old and new, simple and sophisticated, home-brewed and professionally prescribed. You could almost say that in addition to their worn facets, bulging discs, and pinched nerves, the victims of common backache can't seek relief without suffering from a fourth complaint: overchoice.

Hot packs or ice? Traction or massage? Injections or surgery? Everybody you talk to has a different remedy and, usually, a personal testimonial to go with it. How do you sort it all out? First, you have to decide whether you want to treat the cause or simply relieve the pain. No doubt you would like to do both. But when the pain is at its peak, you would settle gratefully for relief alone. And there's nothing the matter with that. After all, it will give you a chance to achieve some comfort and rest while your back goes about the tedious but welcome process of healing itself.

You do want to make sure, however, that the interim remedies you use are safe — free of serious side effects and not injurious. A sound rule to remember is: No home remedy should make you feel worse. And the converse is true: If it feels good, do it.

While it's commendable to apply the power of positive thinking to your personal recovery program, you should never deceive yourself about the value of any remedy. It pays to know, as precisely as you can, how a given remedy is supposed to work, what it can be expected to do for your back, and whether its beneficial effects are likely to last. And in assessing any back treatment, remember that back pain naturally tends to come and go, and that this may occur coincidentally with the application of your therapy, giving you a false impression of its effectiveness. You should be wary, meanwhile, of becoming over-dependent on short-term measures, such as a muscle-relaxant or a back brace. These are poor substitutes for a program of proper, long-term back care.

If you are sincere about plotting a course for your long-term recovery, you should begin by understanding the purpose and worth of each potential remedy. Some are medically proven. Others are based on unproven theories which may or may not be valid. Still others produce limited or erratic results. And there are a few treatments that are patently phony.

Counter-Irritants

Some of the most familiar home remedies are based on the principle of altering your body's perception of pain. This is done by introducing a counter-irritant that causes some new form of pain. No one knows exactly how counter-irritants work. They may release endorphins that relieve pain, or they may jam pain signals so that the body cannot register them fully and accurately.

Hot poultices and *ice packs* are probably the oldest, as well as the commonest, counter-irritants known to man.

Liniments, especially those that feel hot on the skin, are another form of counter-irritant. But don't believe the label on the liniment bottle if it claims that the product will provide "penetrating heat" that gets "deep down into the sore area."

That doesn't happen. Your skin is such an effective insulator that it blocks off any heat or cold that you might apply to your back. Certainly no liniment gets down as far as a facet joint or a disc, and, even if it did, there is no reason to believe that it would make the sore spots feel any better.

Massage, with or without a liniment, may function as a counter-irritant. Or it may help loosen up muscles that have gone into spasm. In cases where a muscle spasm happens to be causing most of the pain, massage may seem to cure a backache entirely, since pain from the original source, such as a worn facet joint, may have subsided in the meantime. You should keep in mind, however, that massage won't cure the trouble that brought on the spasm in the first place. And, of course, if that original condition causes more pain, you may be in for another spasm as well.

Manipulation, too, can be useful in loosening up muscles and joints tightened by a spasm. In fact, that is about all that manipulation is good for, as I pointed out in Chapter Seven. Manipulation doesn't always work, however, and it may hurt, especially if you have a pinched nerve. But hurt, remember, is not the same as harm; ordinarily you can't harm yourself this way. You'll be better off, just the same, if you apply the rule I mentioned earlier: no home remedy should make you feel worse.

The Back Brace

A back brace can be good for you. The trouble is, people often misunderstand why. They assume, erroneously, that a brace wards off pain and helps strengthen your spine. A brace does limit excessive back movement and, more important, it provides essential support for your belly. But even that is a temporary advantage. Without support, weak belly muscles allow your abdomen to sag forward, placing strain on your spine. A brace substitutes for those weak muscles.

The danger, then, is that a brace will become a

crutch. If you rely on it indefinitely, your belly muscles will never grow strong. You are far better off to get started on an exercise program to strengthen those muscles, and meanwhile use a brace only on occasions when you cannot get along without it.

Traction

Traction is one form of treatment that has a more favorable effect on the neck than on the low back. Neck traction can readily stretch the neck and increase the space for the spinal nerves within their exit canals. For this reason it is excellent therapy for Type Three neck pain, an acutely pinched nerve. To be most effective, the traction should be applied most of the time. For severe cases I sometimes recommend seven to ten pounds of pull on the head, with the neck bent forward slightly for one and a half hours out of every two during the day, and continuously at night. I have seen this routine produce dramatic pain relief and even restore function that has been lost through pressure on the nerve. Milder cases of neck pain can benefit from intermittent traction applied three or four times a week during visits to a physiotherapist.

Like any treatment intended to improve a condition without effecting a cure, traction should relieve your symptoms, and it should do so within the first few treatments. Avoid traction if it makes your pain worse. Traction is seldom an effective remedy for people with low-back pain. The size of the trunk, the bulk of the back muscles, and even the shape of the vertebrae make stretching of the lumbar spine extremely difficult.

Some people spend a lot of money on devices consisting of pelvic slings, weights, ropes, and pulleys that purport to make their backs better. Then they lie in bed, letting the apparatus do its thing. As far as I can see, the only beneficial aspect to this treatment is that it induces you to lie down and rest. You could throw away the weights, ropes, and pulleys and achieve just as much simply by lying in bed and allowing your back to get better by itself.

One variation of this treatment is called gravity traction. It uses an apparatus that leaves you hanging vertically, suspended from the chest area, in a sort of Jolly Jumper for grown-ups. Thus, in contrast with traditional, in-bed traction, which provides forty or fifty pounds of pull at the most, gravity traction subjects your spine to the pull exerted by the weight of your entire lower body.

If you are convinced that this latest adaptation of the medieval rack is good for the spine, let me make a suggestion: with a little more effort, but no expense whatever, you can achieve the same effect by suspending yourself by your arms, trapeze-artist style, from any convenient fixture in your house. A door frame or a horizontal overhead water pipe in your basement may do.

Try it. You may like it. But remember, traction for the low back is just one more way of relieving a muscle spasm that might very well go away on its own if you rest your back in the proper position.

The TNS Machine

If this machine didn't already exist, it might have to be invented to satisfy the backache victims who need to spend a lot of money on a magic box. Known both as the Transcutaneous Nerve Stimulation (TNS) machine and the Transcutaneous Electric Nerve Stimulation (TENS) machine, it is no larger than a compact cassette recorder, costs as much as $500, and comes equipped with an impressive assembly of electrical circuits and control buttons. If you have an indulgent doctor, you can obtain a prescription to buy your own TNS machine from a medical supplier. Then, no matter where you are when back pain strikes, you can whip out your machine and zap yourself with electrical impulses.

It's not a fraud. There is good reason to suppose that TNS impulses trigger the release of pain-killing endorphins. Out of every ten people who try TNS for the first time, about seven enjoy beneficial results. Controlled studies on the effectiveness of Transcutaneous Nerve Stimulation are under way in many centers. Its role in the relief of chronic pain of various kinds, including backache, has attracted much medical interest. The trouble is, it's easy to become emotionally dependent on that little black box. Meanwhile, your body becomes resistant to the impulses. And so, the more treatment you take, the more you need. Soon you need more than the machine can deliver. And of course, TNS, even at its best, is just a pain-killer, not a cure. It won't do a thing to your worn facet or your bulging disc.

Worst of all, it encourages the Free Lunch Syndrome — the notion that you can heal your back easily, without expending any time or effort. You delegate your responsibility to the box and it does the job in an instant. Meanwhile, you shun the treatment you really need — the program of long-term care that demands a conscious effort, a degree of discomfort, and a measure of self-discipline.

Mattresses and Car Seats

People with back trouble worry a lot about mattresses. In most cases their worries are unfounded. If you sleep on a good, firm mattress that sits on a standard box spring, you're providing your back with all the help it needs each night. There is no advantage or virtue in sleeping on a hard, uncomfortable surface — unless you enjoy it. The extravagant claims made for waterbeds or special orthopedic mattresses are based on the simple fact that they supply contoured support for the back to maintain it in a neutral position.

Forget the old idea of a rigid board under the

mattress. That idea had merit at one time. But those were the days when beds consisted of link springs and stuffed mattresses that sagged like a sway-backed horse on its way to the glue factory. A bed like that provided virtually no support for your spine, and in that situation a rigid board made sense. If your mattress feels comfortable when your back is pain-free, forget about adding any refinements, homemade or otherwise.

No matter what sort of mattress you use, you'll probably be more comfortable during times of back pain if you lie on your back with a fat pillow under your knees, or on your side with your knees bent and a pillow between your thighs.

There is no magic formula for the ideal car seat, either. But one basic principle is important: keep your knees higher than your hips. That means positioning your car seat as close as possible to the steering wheel — within the bounds of safety and comfort, of course. This position causes you to bend your legs and reduce the strain on your back. For comfort and good visibility, you may want to sit on a wedge-shaped cushion or place one behind your back. But let common sense prevail: whatever arrangement reduces your back pain is the right arrangement for you.

All these remedies fall into the same category. With the exception of those common-sense practices with mattresses and car seats, they offer no lasting benefits, but they cause no immediate harm, either.

On the other hand, professional treatments offering long-term relief, though not harmful, vary enormously in quality. They range from the medically proven to the patently fraudulent. And between those two extremes lie many whose results are limited or unpredictable. First, a quick look at a typical fraud.

Useless Injections

Sad to say, it sometimes seems that if you look hard enough you can find some doctor who will inject you

with almost anything — just short of what's lethal —
in the guise of treatment for your back. Such injections
include sugar, salt water (dignified as "hypertonic
saline"), and phenol (alias carbolic acid). There is not a
shred of scientific evidence to prove that any of these
substances will help your back, either by relieving
pain or by promoting healing — except, of course, by
creating the Placebo Effect, which I discussed in
Chapter Seven.

The proponents of such injections, however, are not
easily troubled by their lack of scientific backing.
They have their own theories. Injecting sugar into the
spinal area, for example, is said to "tighten the
ligaments" by causing inflammation that "scars down
the joint and tightens it up." But nobody has ever
established that back problems are caused by "loose
joints" or that a back will get better if those joints are
"tightened." Anyway, inflammation doesn't cause
tightening. Rather, it creates damage that makes
ligaments loose.

But never mind. Those injections cost hundreds of
dollars — paid by patients who reason that if something is expensive it must be good. A few doctors
willing to nurture that notion are making a full-time
specialty out of these worthless injections.

Now let's look at a few of the treatments producing
responses that are limited or unpredictable — in most
cases because the physiology of the treatment is not
completely understood. Two forms of therapy that fall
into this category — acupuncture and chiropractic —
were discussed earlier. Here are some others.

Muscle Relaxants

As I often tell patients in my Back Education classes,
there are no such things as muscle relaxants — only
people relaxants. No matter what they're called, they
can't be directed at a specific group of muscles. Taken
orally, they have to relax the whole person.

If your doctor prescribes one of these drugs for you

he may call it by a generic name (diazepam is one of the most widely used) or a trade name, such as Valium (which is one brand of diazepam). But you may not like the idea of relaxing your whole body, especially if you are an active person. It's hard to keep going when your brain feels as though it's covered with fuzz. Another drawback is that muscle relaxants aren't pain-relievers — not directly anyway. About all that a relaxant can do for your back is loosen up a muscle spasm — assuming you have one — and thus indirectly reduce your pain.

Anti-inflammatory Drugs

Inflammation could be described as a speeded-up version of what is happening in your body all the time, with cells coming and going, forming and dying. Anti-inflammatories are drugs that slow an abnormally rapid process down to a normal pace. Aspirin in high dosages is probably the best known and most widely used anti-inflammatory of them all. The anti-inflammatories commonly prescribed by doctors fall into two classes: steroids and non-steroidal anti-inflammatory drugs.

Steroids, such as cortisone, may be taken by mouth for a general effect or injected into muscles, discs, or joints to reduce local inflammation. There is no doubt that cortisone is capable of reducing inflammation, but the desired pain relief does not always occur. One reason may be that the pain is caused not by inflammation but by a mechanical condition, such as the worn surfaces of a facet joint rubbing together. Even when inflammation is apparently the cause of pain, the cortisone may not work. Whenever a disc presses against a nerve, a complex chemical reaction takes place. The cortisone may take care of the inflammation but leave the remaining chemistry of pain unaffected.

Even in instances where cortisone does reduce pain, it is only a stopgap measure, since it does nothing to remedy the cause of the pain. But stopgaps can be worthwhile if they are recognized and employed for what they are.

Non-steroidal Anti-inflammatory Drugs (NSAID) tend to offer an all-or-nothing proposition. When they work, they work well; in other cases they seem to have no effect. Their success varies widely from patient to patient and even from one time to another for the same patient.

There are many non-steroidal drugs to choose from, and some enjoy a period of popularity and then fall out of favor. Two that have been around a long time and remain popular are phenylbutazone and indomethacin (both generic names). Phenylbutazone is an excellent anti-inflammatory, but it should not be used for extended periods because it can have serious side effects on a patient's blood. Indomethacin is an excellent drug for treating osteoarthritis, but it can cause headaches and stomach upsets.

Two currently popular non-steroidals are naproxen and ibuprofen. Both are said to provide good anti-inflammatory action without serious side effects. Neither of them, however, can be relied upon to produce uniformly beneficial effects in any large group of back patients. Like steroids, NSAIDS can relieve pain caused by inflammation but can do nothing to remedy mechanical problems caused by aging.

Ultrasound

This is a modified version of the microwave oven. It can do one thing you can't do with your hot-water bottles, poultices, or liniments: it can beam heat right into your body, well below the surface of your skin. And that may ease the pain in your spine. Or it may not. The whole idea, you see, is based on two assumptions — both of them unproven. One assumption is that the heat generated by ultrasound will actually

reach the affected area. Nobody can say for sure that it
will. The second assumption is that heat eases pain.
We know that heat causes blood vessels to expand and
extra blood to accumulate. But does extra blood ease
pain? Nobody knows. All we know, really, is that
sometimes ultrasound helps a bad back feel better —
at least for a while.

Chemonucleolysis

Translated from Doctor, chemonucleolysis means a
chemical destruction of the disc center. Currently this
is a most controversial form of back treatment.

Chemonucleolysis is practised in many countries,
including Canada, the United Kingdom, France, Australia, Poland, and the Soviet Union — but not in the
United States. There the drug involved has been
withdrawn by the supplier and its use is not permitted.
This action was taken following a study showing the
results of chemonucleolysis to be no better than the
Placebo Effect. Ever since, doctors in Canada have
been administering this treatment to a steady stream
of back patients from the United States. This treatment, intended to relieve the pressure exerted on a
nerve by a bulging disc, consists of injecting the disc
with an enzyme called chymopapain, which is related
to the enzyme used in those meat tenderizers you
sprinkle on tough steaks. Injected into a bulging disc,
chymopapain apparently denatures the protein, thereby drying out the nuclear material.

Many doctors doubt whether the enzyme can do
what it is purported to do. Chemonucleolysis can be a
painful treatment even when administered under
heavy sedation, but it takes less time and causes less
aggravation and pain than surgery, which is often the
alternative.

Unfortunately, chemonucleolysis is unpredictable,
sometimes providing relief within minutes, at other
times not for weeks. The success of chymopapain in

the treatment of acute disc herniation is claimed to be about seventy percent.

A chymopapain injection has side effects. The most serious is an allergic reaction that could be fatal. This reaction, however, is immediately evident, making the risk very slight for any patient under competent medical supervision.

My own opinion of disc injection is that it's safe enough but is useful only in treating a patient who has a herniated disc pressing on a nerve. It is of no use to patients with facet problems (Type One) or simple discogenic pain (Type Two).

Rhizotomy

Also known as rhizolysis, this treatment has become popular with some doctors. The terms mean "to cut or destroy a nerve root." This operation involves cutting the nerves to the facet joints. It sounds perfectly logical: since the facet is the commonest source of back pain, depriving the joint of its ability to feel pain should cure your trouble. But the theory doesn't always work out in practice. Your body is not deterred that easily from doing its normal job of transmitting nerve sensations. When one route is cut off, another is used. The operation may be a complete success — except that the patient's back still hurts. In some cases, the surgeon simply fails to cut all the nerves involved. In an attempt to make it more effective, the original surgical approach has been replaced largely by the destruction of nerves by means of either a radio-frequency probe or thermal or chemical means. Even with these newer techniques, only four out of ten rhizotomies are successful.

At the beginning of this chapter I remarked on the wide range of choices open to any patient in search of a remedy for back pain. Like most back doctors, I hope that as we learn more about the physiology and pathology of back problems, many of the inconsistent and limited treatments will be made reliable and more effective, and that, with better understanding, the worthless "cures" will disappear.

At the moment, however, reliable, medically proven remedies, beyond those used for short-term pain relief, are limited to a group of standard surgical procedures, plus the conservative treatment — the exercise, the good postural habits, and the improved life-style — on which the philosophy of this book is based.

As you will learn in the next chapter, surgery is not "the ultimate" in back treatment but merely a means of helping to correct certain conditions that arise in the spines of a minority of back patients. And, as you will see from later chapters, surgery is no substitute for a lifelong program of sensible back care.

10 Surgery: When, Why, and How?

To many people with back problems, spinal surgery is magic — the cure-all for any condition too serious to be remedied by some "lesser" treatment.

That belief, however, has no basis in reality. For one thing, it ignores the fact that surgery is capable of helping only a fraction of all backache victims. And, among the relative few who can benefit from surgery, it encourages unrealistic expectations of a complete, lifelong cure.

Ironically, the concept of surgery as a cure-all is sometimes nurtured by doctors themselves. In a well-meaning attempt to encourage a positive attitude towards an impending operation, a surgeon may speak too glibly of "getting you all fixed up" or "taking care of your disc trouble."

It sounds straightforward. But no back operation can be unconditionally guaranteed. And even if it could, your back problems would not necessarily be over for all time. Some disc or joint that never caused trouble before could start hurting next week or next year. In any case, spinal surgery can't really cure a bad back — at least not in the sense that an appendectomy can cure appendicitis. Spinal surgery can correct a specific mechanical condition, such as a bulging disc pressing against a nerve. But in doing so, it will leave you with a back that is something less than normal. A normal back, as I have said before, doesn't have a scar on it. And, whatever condition is being corrected, you are almost certain to come out with some part of your spine removed or some once-movable joint perma-

nently immobilized. In fact, as we'll see later in this
chapter, the alterations that take place in your spine
during surgery may even cause or contribute to new
back trouble at some time in the future. I'm not
opposed to spinal surgery. On the contrary, I perform
back operations frequently. What I am saying is that
surgery has limitations that many back patients fail to
appreciate.

Patients also fail, sometimes, to understand why a
doctor will recommend surgery in a given case. They'll
tell their friends, "My back was so painful he just had
to operate." Actually, the degree of pain has little to do
with the decision to operate. There is also a widely
held notion that surgery is a means of "getting it all
over with quickly" and avoiding the need for further
back care. The fact is that when you are left with a
less-than-normal back, you will have more reason
than ever to keep it in condition with exercise and
proper living habits.

In deciding whether to operate, your doctor must
answer one basic question: "Does this patient have a
condition that can be — and should be — corrected by
surgery?" In other words, surgery is not a substitute
for other forms of treatment; like any other, it should
be used when it is the most appropriate treatment in
the circumstances, and it should be rejected when it
is not.

Whenever that point seems to have escaped one of
my patients, I draw the analogy of the sick tree. If
something is ailing a favorite tree in your front yard,
you wouldn't expect to make it well automatically by
lopping off a branch or two. You'd try to find out what
was wrong and apply the appropriate remedy, whether
it was a splint to heal a serious break, or a wire fence to
protect the bark from hungry rabbits. You'd use
surgery only when surgery was the best or only
solution. Often I extend the analogy to emphasize the
need for long-term care. I point out that the immediate
remedy for that tree would be no substitute for its

continuing needs — water, fertilizer, sunlight, and space in which to grow.

As long as you realize that surgery is just one step in the lifelong management of your back, you are unlikely to be disappointed by the results of an operation. In many cases, surgery produces some exciting results, such as the instant relief of pain, following the removal of a large fragment of disc from a nerve root. But it is a mistake to think of spinal surgery as a measure that will inevitably end in either triumph or tragedy. Usually the outcome will lie somewhere between those two extremes.

Having acquired realistic expectations, you can increase your chances of success even more by learning everything you can about the physical aspects of your operation: why surgery is a good idea in your case, how you can prepare yourself for it, what your doctor will do in the operating room, how you'll feel afterwards, and what you can do to help ensure a speedy recovery. Chances are, you will have plenty of time to learn everything you need to know. For, with the exception of central disc herniation, which I described in Chapter Eight, a decision to operate on your spine won't be made overnight. Or let me put it another way: if your doctor makes a snap decision about surgery for you, I suggest you request a second opinion from another surgeon.

About two years ago, a forty-three-year-old warehouseman came to me from another doctor who had recommended surgery. My new patient had wrenched his back while lifting a heavy food carton in a supermarket warehouse. By the time I saw him, he had been back on the job for two months. But occasionally his spine still hurt, especially at the end of a day's work.

His first doctor — call him Dr. J. — had X-rayed his back and produced a diagnosis that I believe was accurate: the man had spondylolysis. That's the condition where two small breaks in the back of a vertebra have occurred and failed to mend. The result is an abnormal separation between the upper and lower sets of joints on the back of that one bone. Research has shown that this condition usually appears before the age of five. My patient, then, had had these defects in his spine for more than thirty-five years. Yet he had never had back pain until the day of that minor accident in the warehouse.

I'm sure Dr. J. would agree with me that those were the facts of the case. But on the question of surgery we parted company. Dr. J. believed that fusion was an urgent necessity, to bring stability to those separated joints.

That isn't the way I saw it. Here was a man whose spondylolysis had given him no trouble whatever for thirty-five years or more. Now his first attack of pain was subsiding and could probably be remedied entirely if someone showed him the basics of conservative care. In my opinion, surgery was hardly necessary, let alone urgent.

What's more, the patient himself didn't want the operation. He was more than willing to try a program of exercise and proper care — something he had never done before. And so that's what I prescribed for him. At this writing, he is still at it, and doing well. He has everything to gain and nothing to lose. If the care program is effective, he will never need surgery. On the other hand, if surgery proves to be necessary after all, he will be well prepared for it — thoroughly briefed and trained in the self-help that is vital in the post-operative period.

His situation brings to mind another misconception people often have about back treatment. Patients assume that when a surgeon declines to operate, there is nothing more he can do for them. Actually, he can provide several other major services. He can examine your back and diagnose your problem. He can direct the conservative management of your back. He can prescribe medication for you. He can organize and supervise physiotherapy. And he can monitor your condition, conducting additional examinations and altering the diagnosis and treatment whenever it seems wise to do so.

The limitations of surgery become clear once you learn that there are only two basic kinds of operations for coping with common back trouble. One involves decompression; the other, stabilization.

In plainer English, decompression means relieving the pressure that part of the spine is exerting on the spinal nerves. There are two types of patients who require decompressive surgery — those with a disc pressing on a nerve, and those with a nerve being squeezed by the bone itself. Most often a bulging disc is responsible for pressure on a nerve, typically against a nerve root where it leaves the spine. This is the most common cause of Type Three back pain. Less commonly, the disc presses against the dural sac, the sheath encasing the nerves within the spinal canal. Or, as we saw earlier, a piece of the disc may break away and lodge against a nerve. In other cases where decompression is required, the culprit is not a disc but a bony prominence that is squeezing down on a nerve or closing the canal. Surgery here removes the offending portion of bone and opens the space around the nerve.

Surgery to relieve disc pressure entails removal of part of the disc. This operation is known conventionally (but not accurately) as a disc removal or, in Doctor, a discotomy. Removal of bone covering the nerve is termed a laminectomy. Since "-tomy" means "to cut," "discotomy" means "to cut a disc." And since "-ectomy" means "the operative removal of," "laminectomy" means the operative removal of the lamina, the roof of the spinal canal. Most of the back operations I perform are either discotomies or laminectomies. (Incidentally, if part of the bone on the back of the spinal canal is cut away just to allow room for the removal of a bulging disc, the operation gains the impressive title of laminectomy-discotomy.) Micro-discotomy is a term describing the surgical removal of a portion of a disc with the aid of an operating microscope. There is nothing wrong with this technique, but I believe a good surgeon can do his job just as well with a conventional pair of magnifying glasses or with the naked eye.

Stabilization means eliminating movement in one or more joints. This is done by a process called fusion — that is, joining together bones on either side of the joint. Typically, fusion is performed at the level of a protruding intervertebral disc and badly worn facet joints, where movement is painful and the joints are not healing properly by themselves. Occasionally more than one level may be fused, but the risk of failure increases with each additional level.

Whenever he decides to operate for common back trouble, a surgeon will always have either decompression or stabilization as his objective. Although you may hear someone with back trouble talking about having an exploratory operation, it is not quite as it sounds. Before he operates, a surgeon can usually learn all he needs to know about your back problem from your history, your physical examination, and whatever X-rays and tests are appropriate. No competent surgeon will open your back just to poke around in search of trouble, although he may need to explore one small area to actually see the problem. No incision can provide a view of more than a fraction of your total spine. By the time he takes scalpel in hand, your surgeon has to know exactly where he's going and what to expect when he gets there.

By now you may be wondering what convinces a doctor that one particular back patient needs a surgical decompression when so many others don't. One important clue is the patient's failure to respond to conservative management — rest, exercise, and proper habits. I would judge this not from the pain the patient describes but from the persistence of weaknesses in his muscles, loss of reflexes, and decreased sensation in parts of his legs.

Surgery is also called for when a patient has a neurological defect that could be described as either massive or progressive. I call a defect massive if, for example, the person has lost all power to stand on tiptoe because he is unable to move his foot downwards. And certainly I would call a defect progressive if a minor weakness developed into a major one in only a few weeks' time, despite proper bed rest. It's rare to see either a massive or a progressive neurological defect, but when either appears, I recommend early surgery.

Sometimes I conclude that surgery is necessary when I see a patient who responds to conservative management for a few months but who continues to suffer repeated attacks of back pain and loss of function in the same muscles or nerves each time. The decision to operate in this case is a judgment call on my part. It is based on my assessment of the disruption of the patient's life by the recurrent attacks and by my opinion of the patient's ability to cope with each episode of back pain. That's unscientific, I know, but much of healing is still an art, not a science, and sometimes there is nothing better than sound clinical judgment based on experience.

Apart from specific diseases and serious back injuries (which this book is not intended to cover), the only other condition that would prompt me to undertake decompressive back surgery is central disc herniation. This is the extremely rare condition I described in Chapter Eight: a protruding disc exerts pressure on several nerves inside the spinal canal. This is the only diagnosis in the realm of low-back pain that may require an immediate operation.

Let us suppose that you are a patient of mine in need of a discotomy. Here's what you can expect.

You will have most of your tests as an out-patient. Perhaps only the myelogram will be done after your

admission to hospital for surgery. On the afternoon
before your surgery, you come into hospital to be
examined and have your history taken by one of the
hospital doctors, who will order routine blood and
urine tests. You may receive pre-operative instruction
from the nursing staff, and the skin of your back will
be prepared. The night before your operation, you will
be given a sedative and instructed to take nothing to
eat or drink by mouth after midnight.

On the morning of your surgery you will be given a
needle to relax you before you are transferred to the
operating room. There you are put under a general
anesthetic and positioned face down on the operating
table. Now you can breathe easily and your back is
readily accessible.

I begin your discotomy by making a two-inch
incision over your spine in your low back. Then I work
my way slowly downwards by moving through or
around the various layers of muscle, bone, and ligament I encounter along the way. After removing one
small part of the roof of the spinal canal, I arrive at the
nerve root and finally the disc.

If there are any loose fragments of disc evident, I
remove them. I look for the weak spot or hole I know
will be found in the shell of the disc, much like a
blowout in a tire, from which some of the contents may
have escaped. I enlarge the hole and then use a
specially designed instrument to remove the rest of the
contents of that one offending disc. I will leave the disc
empty, confident that over the next several weeks the
space will become partly and painlessly occupied by
scar tissue.

Withdrawal is much easier than the entry was: I
simply replace the nerve root and muscles that have
been temporarily pushed aside, bring the incision
together, and stitch up the skin.

The whole operation, from opening to closing, takes
about an hour.

You are taken to the recovery room, where you

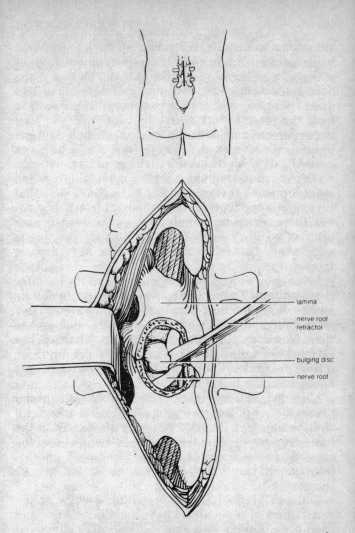

Fig. 14. Drawn to scale, this illustration represents the surgeon's view of the back during a disc operation. With a small part of the roof removed, little is visible within the spinal canal except a single nerve root and the bulging portion of the disc.

regain consciousness. When most of the effects of the anesthetic have worn off, you are returned to your own room in the hospital. For the next twelve hours the nurses make sure you stay on your back as much as you can. The weight of your body provides pressure to keep the wound from oozing.

For a couple of days, at least, your back is quite painful. As long as the pain lasts you will be given pain-killers. The discomfort will come mainly from your back muscles, which were unavoidably bruised when I pushed them aside. But soon you realize that this new pain represents a good trade-off. It's not nearly so sharp or troublesome as the pain from a pinched nerve. That horrible pain down your leg is gone. And, best of all, the pain you have now is temporary.

I want you up and walking as soon as possible after the operation. You will be encouraged to get up for the bathroom even on the same night. On the second day after your operation you should be up much of the time. You may find, though, that your stomach has stopped working. I don't want you to eat anything during the first day or two, until your digestive tract is functioning normally again.

Most people are surprised to find that no special precautions are necessary to keep their backs from "falling apart." I do ask you not to sit, except in the bathroom, for the first few weeks. Sitting pulls on the skin stitches and may cause local bleeding. Standing, leaning, or lying down are much easier on the soft tissues.

You can probably go home within a week or ten days. Some of my patients have had discotomies and been back in their own homes in only five days.

At home, you need extra rest. And of course you should temporarily avoid placing extra stress on your back. After two weeks or so, scar tissue will have toughened things up and you can begin to move and sit more freely.

No special appliances, equipment, or therapy are necessary during your convalescence. Your own bed is fine. You won't wear a brace. You don't have to visit a physiotherapist. Depending on what you do for a living, you may go back to work in four to six weeks after the operation.

Perhaps the best news of all is that your discotomy is the least disruptive to your system of any kind of major back surgery, and it has a ninety-percent chance of being a complete success — no more pain or trouble from that disc.

I said earlier that decompression operations don't necessarily involve discs. Especially in older patients, the bone of the vertebra itself can exert pressure on a nerve root. It may be an unusually narrow spinal canal or the partial closing of the nerve's exit between two adjacent vertebrae. In some cases, a bone spur on the edge of a facet joint may press the nerve against the floor of the exit canal.

Another variation occurs after a disc has narrowed and allowed the vertebrae to settle together more closely than normal. This creates an abnormally sharp angle in the nerve at its point of exit. The result is the same sort of pinching effect that occurs when you try to haul a garden hose around the corner of your house.

Nerve pressure may develop in people whose spinal canal has grown too narrow from the natural bony overgrowth of aging or has never developed to normal size in the first place. In either case, the nerves of the canal have no room, and the cramped quarters reduce their supply of blood, making it impossible for the patient to walk more than a short distance without stopping to rest.

With all these various conditions, the general surgical approach is a decompression operation of the same type as for a herniated disc. The surgeon removes a section of bone or enlarges an exit canal, depending on what is exerting pressure on the nerve, but he usually leaves the discs intact. In a case of spinal-canal narrowing, all the laminae and large portions of the facet joints may be removed at two or more levels of the spine.

If you were to have one of these bony decompression operations, your routine during recovery and convalescence would likely be the same as after a standard discotomy, though the pace would be slower. If a great amount of bone had been removed, I would order you to wear a back brace for several weeks, until I was confident that your spine had regained enough strength to manage on its own.

Fusions of two or more vertebrae are performed less frequently than simple decompressions. As a rule, a number of factors must come together before I will recommend fusion for any patient. Fusion, you see, is usually a judgment call. Before I perform a fusion on anyone, I have to be convinced that the person is in serious pain that is unlikely to subside, and that he is virtually disabled.

The patient's attitude and past record must also be right. I must be convinced that he has made a serious, prolonged attempt to remedy his condition through a proper program of exercise and good living habits. He must realize that fusion won't make his spine normal. He must acknowledge the importance of post-operative care — indefinitely. He must be prepared to accept a degree of post-operative discomfort, if not pain. If he comes to me with a mild backache and wants fusion so that he'll have no backache at all, I can't help him. And, finally, he must have confidence in me as his surgeon. He must believe that what I do will make him feel better, even though I can't offer to cure him.

If we're lucky, the problem will prove to be confined to a single level. That way, our chances of success are greatest. If only a single level has to be fused, we have a ninety-percent chance of fusing it successfully. If two levels are fused at the same operation, the percentage drops to roughly seventy-five. With three levels, we're down to a success rate of less than fifty percent.

It's a matter of simple mechanics: the greater the length of spine involved, the less chance we have of immobilizing it entirely against the stress of normal movement.

If wear and tear has damaged more than three levels, the problem is beyond surgical correction. In other circumstances, such as in cases of spinal curvature (scoliosis), surgeons sometimes fuse as many as eight or ten levels. Such operations, however, call for a quite different technique, involving the use of long metal rods or a tension cable inserted into the spine. These techniques have been developed for these special conditions. They are not used to remedy mechanical wear and tear, which, if extensive, cannot be corrected even by the most drastic forms of surgery.

Let's suppose now that you are a patient who is to undergo a spinal fusion. Here's what happens. You go through the same preliminaries as you would for a discotomy, and I begin with essentially the same kind of incision, except that it is longer. I clear away more muscles and other material than I would to treat a disc, and I thoroughly clean off the backs of the vertebrae that are to be fused.

Now I roughen the exposed surfaces of these vertebrae with an instrument resembling a double-beveled chisel. This deliberate damage activates the bones' healing response and leads to fusion.

Now, through either the same incision or a separate one, I expose the back of your pelvis, which will provide me with the extra bone I need. I carve off little strips of bone a bit thicker than matchsticks, each about an inch long.

When I have collected a dozen or more of these bone sticks, I pack them on either side of the vertebrae to be fused.

In roughening the back surfaces of the vertebrae, I trick the body into reacting as though a fracture had occurred. The body's healing mechanism incorporates the newly placed sticks of bone into the spine, as though they are parts of vertebrae that have broken away. If the fusion works as well as it should, these bone sticks will soon be united with the vertebrae, immobilizing them into a single bone.

As I withdraw from the site, I replace any muscles that have been pushed aside, then close this incision as I would any other. If I have made a separate incision at the pelvis, I of course close it too.

During the post-operative period, your spine has to be treated more delicately than it would after a discotomy. While fusion does not involve as many sensitive parts of the spine, it depends for its success on your ability to keep the newly fused joints reasonably undisturbed. Those strips of bone need time to unite with the vertebrae. That doesn't mean treating your back as though it were rare porcelain, but you do have to wear a low-back brace and move around carefully. If your back requires extreme protection, perhaps after an attempt to fuse several levels, you would be nursed on a circle-electric bed or on the more old-fashioned turning frame. These are both devices that allow you to be rolled over onto your stomach without your doing the moving. The bed or the frame does all the work.

Unless you require special protection, you will stay in hospital about two weeks and spend another two and a half months recovering at home. You will be up and around during that time, but you will be obliged to restrict your activity to movements unlikely to disturb the fusion.

Ironically, the sorest part of your body is often not the site of the fusion but the donor site — that area in your pelvic bone where those "matchsticks" were obtained.

Occasionally I perform a spinal fusion in the low back by operating from the front of the patient's body. This may be necessary if a solid fusion cannot be achieved from behind; for example, when previous surgery has removed most of the bony covering over

he spinal cord and there is no way of positioning the
"matchsticks" used in the graft. The approach from the
ront allows me to remove much of the disc and pack
he space between the vertebrae with bone sticks I
lave obtained from the pelvis.

Surgery from the front of the spine is standard for
operations on discs in the cervical or neck area. This
approach is used for the neck because, unlike the low
back, where nerves in the spinal canal can be pushed
aside to allow access to a bulging disc, the cervical
spine contains a section of the spinal cord which
cannot be moved. Discotomy in the neck is routinely
combined with fusion because this part of the spine
might otherwise become unstable.

Many patients assume that a fusion will make their
backs stronger than normal. In fact, fusion simply
makes your back more rigid — and not even as
effectively so as nature does more gradually and more
subtly. Fusion is an awkward arrangement which
inevitably increases the strain on the unfused levels
nearby. This extra load can lead to problems in the
future. And, as we saw, the greater the number of
vertebrae fused, the greater the chance of failure
through mechanical stress. You may be asked to
consider having a fusion for common back pain from
wear and tear on a facet or disc. The more levels your
surgeon wants to fuse, the more skeptical you should
be, and the more inclined to seek a second opinion.

Whether you have had a stabilization or a decompression, the time may come when your doctor recommends a second operation on your spine. If that
happens, you have every right to know why. The key
question is: Is this a new problem, or are we just trying
to correct trouble left over from the first time? Here are
some explanations you may hear and my comments.

"The same disc is causing trouble again."

This doesn't happen often. A thorough cleanout of
the disc should eliminate herniation at the same level

on the same side. Because it is an uncommon complication, I'd ask the opinion of another surgeon before agreeing to further surgery.

"A different disc has herniated."

This is nobody's fault — just bad luck. If conservative management doesn't yield results, surgery may be the only solution. This is also true if the same disc has now herniated on the opposite side and is affecting the opposite leg.

"Your problem is that there's scarring on the nerve root."

Maybe your surgeon could have prevented the scarring, and maybe he couldn't. The scarring may have come from surgery, or it might have been caused by the original disc pressure. But surgery won't necessarily solve the problem. If your surgeon cuts the scar away, another will likely form.

"That same nerve is being pinched again. Last time the disc was to blame; this time it's the bone."

This is plausible. When a disc loses some of its contents and height, the vertebrae come together more closely and the nerve exit is narrowed. A portion of the bone may be pressing down on the nerve. Your doctor may recommend either a bony decompression to relieve the pressure, or a fusion to prevent further narrowing of the joint. Or both. But don't blame your first operation for your new trouble; it might have occurred anyway.

"The fusion didn't hold."

Although you followed your doctor's orders after the operation, there is a ten-percent chance that even a one-level fusion will fail. But before you consent to a second attempt at fusing the same level, make sure you receive clear and positive answers to these three questions: 1. Has my fusion really failed, or is it only

11 Can You Spare
Ten Minutes a Day?

How would you like to know that you will never have another moment of serious worry about back pain?

That may sound like the sort of opening you would hear from some snake-oil salesman making a pitch for Professor Hamilton Hall's Miraculous Elixir for Bad Backs. But that's hardly what I'm selling. I am talking not about curing back pain but about controlling it and no longer fearing it. And certainly there are no miracles involved in my method. In fact its most obvious weakness — if you can call it that — lies in its most undramatic simplicity. It is so simple that many people refuse, at first, to believe that it works.

But it does work. I know, because over the past several years I have seen its results among thousands of people who have come to our Back Education classes and discovered how to manage their back problems, reducing their pain and overcoming their fears.

If they can achieve those results, so can you. You can begin, as they did, by recognizing that common backache is not a disease but a sign of the normal wear and tear that accompanies growth and maturity — like gray hair. Obviously, if you didn't want the gray in your hair to show, you wouldn't go around looking for a cure for aging or for graying; you would accept the inevitability of it all and apply treatments to control your hair color. Similarly, if your back is suffering from the wear and tear of aging, you would be wise to accept your condition as inescapable, forget about finding a cure, and go to work on treatments that will enable you to control the pain.

You will soon discover that conservative management does not mean sparing your back at all costs and behaving like an invalid. It means taking charge of your spinal resources — building them up and then expending them as you see fit, to suit your individual wants and needs. How do you lay the groundwork? By adopting the three measures I call the Triple A attack on back pain.

Abdominal exercises

In only ten minutes a day, you can begin strengthening the muscles that serve and protect your spine. Gradually you will reduce your chances of having a serious attack of back pain. Later in this chapter you will be offered a wide assortment of exercises from which to choose those that suit your needs.

Since many back-sparing techniques impose an added strain on leg muscles that may be unaccustomed to it, you might want to add a couple of thigh-strengthening exercises to your regular routine. They are also described later.

Activities of daily living

We call these simply ADL. They demand a change of life-style, but no sacrifice, on your part. You learn how to carry yourself and use your body in dozens of everyday situations — at work, play, recreation, and rest. Soon, the comfortable way becomes more natural for you than the pain-producing way. The principles of ADL are more fully explained in Chapter Thirteen.

Attitude

Nothing is more important than understanding your back problem, knowing how to cope with an attack and becoming confident that there is no longer anything to fear.

As I said, the program is simple. But it is not effortless. If you want to control your back problem instead of allowing it to control you, you must expend some effort. You must do the exercises faithfully every day, and you must make good postural habits as routine as brushing your teeth or tying your shoelaces.

Many doctors and physiotherapists feel that other exercise programs, particularly extension exercises or muscle-stretching routines, are just as valuable as the abdominal-flexion program given here. As with everything else about simple back control, there are no inside secrets. If extension or stretching is prescribed for you and it works, keep it up — but stick to a regular routine of about ten minutes a day. You must be patient, and you must persevere. Forget about overnight results and medical miracles. Settle in for a long haul. Don't worry: there will be a payoff, but it will take time — usually two or three months.

Adopting the right attitude does not mean brainwashing yourself. Rather, it means understanding the realities of back pain and knowing the appropriate responses. It's important, for example, to expect bad days as well as good ones and to treat the bad days for what they are — just momentary setbacks, not the beginning of a steady decline.

And you must expect new attacks of back pain. But once you are prepared for them, you can look forward to reducing their severity and duration. If you used to have two attacks per year, you may well continue to have two attacks per year. But it's unlikely that your future attacks will be the "killers" that once prodded you with pain for a month or more. Instead, you may reduce them to mild attacks that are gone in a few days.

Although we speak of this program of self-treatment as conservative management, it is based on a philosophy of permissiveness. It may sound strange to hear someone talking about conservative treatment in one breath and permissiveness in the next, but the two actually fit together perfectly in this program. The idea is that you learn only principles and guidelines, not rules. It's up to you to decide what you want to do to conserve your spinal resources and how you want to expend them. The process is like putting money into a savings account and then budgeting the funds according to your needs, wants, or whims. Every time you exercise certain muscles or adopt a certain healthy stance, you're making a "deposit" in your "back account." Every time you subject your spine to unusual strain or fail to exercise it, you're making a "withdrawal."

Sometimes you may feel it's worthwhile to make a deliberate withdrawal — to endure a little pain in return for the advantage of carrying out a necessary task or a favorite activity. And why not? It won't harm you; at the worst, it may just leave your back feeling sore for a day or two. You're probably better off playing in that golf tournament next Sunday and collecting a little back pain than you would be sitting at home missing the fun and feeling sorry for yourself. And on Christmas Day, go ahead and give a piggyback ride to that favorite small nephew or grandchild you haven't seen for a year; you may never get another chance, and he's worth a little discomfort, isn't he?

I take that attitude with me onto the basketball court. I've had Type Two back pain since I was a teenager, but I love basketball. I know that every time I play the game my back will be stressed repeatedly, and I know perfectly well my back will be sore afterwards. But so what? Hurt is not the same as harm. To me, it's a price worth paying for a good workout on the court — a fair trade-off that I make willingly. Perhaps you'll want to think a little more about trade-offs of your own, especially when you read Chapter Thirteen and see the effects various sports have on sore backs.

The exercise portion of our back-management program is specialized. Unlike a general fitness routine that conditions your various muscles and organs from head to toe, our plan is designed strictly to provide you with good control of your back. Fitness is important, and I recommend a general exercise program to anyone who is interested. Back exercise is not the same thing, and substitutions are not acceptable. If you want to work out two hours a day, fine; but be sure that ten minutes of that time is set aside for your back program. That way, if fitness becomes a bore and the two hours are put to a different use, your back exercises stand a better chance of remaining a part of your daily routine.

Abdominal exercises, the most important, strengthen your belly muscles to provide your spine with the additional support it needs. Two supplementary types of exercise are also suggested: *neck exercises* will help control chronic neck pain or help ward off new neck pain that might develop, ironically, from your abdominal exercises; *thigh exercises* prepare your legs for the new habits of posture and movement you adopt to avoid straining your spine.

Before you attempt a program of back exercise, make sure you understand its purpose. Exercise is a means of developing control of your back and helping to prevent acute attacks that would otherwise occur in the future. Exercise is not a means of overcoming an acute attack that has already occurred; for that, the proper remedy is rest. Exercise also plays an essential role in controlling the chronic pain that occurs with Type One back trouble (the worn facet joint) and Type Two (the bulging disc). Only a very few exercises are suitable, however, for Type Three pain (pressure on a nerve). Type Three is usually resolved through rest but may require additional medical treatment, perhaps surgery. And remember: exercise is only one prong of the Triple A attack. No one should expect to remain free of back pain with just ten minutes of back exercise a day.

Before you recoil at the sight of these first seventeen exercises which are designed to strengthen your abdomen, take note that nobody is suggesting that you should attempt them all. Keep in mind that this is a permissive program, and what you are offered here is a wide selection of exercises from which to choose a few that suit your needs. The routines that follow are just examples of programs you might adopt, depending on your personal circumstances. I think of many of them as exercises for people who hate exercise — but who presumably hate back pain even more.

While some exercises are harder than others, it would be wrong to describe any as better than others. "Better" depends entirely on your experience and your needs. What you should be looking for are at least three — or as many as six — exercises that keep your back feeling good. Don't feel guilty if you pick several of the easiest; if they work, they're right for you. And don't feel any obligation to progress from easy exercises to difficult ones. As long as those you choose are helping your back, you can stay with them indefinitely.

The first seventeen exercises on our list have been selected because they are likely to do the most good and cause the least pain for the greatest number of backache victims. They are all exercises that strengthen the belly muscles, which in most people are badly out of shape, and they are unlikely to cause pain for people with Type One back trouble — worn facet joints — who make up the majority of back patients. I recommend a flexion, abdomen-strengthening routine because I have found it most efficient. But any regular back exercise is better than none at all.

Regardless of the exercises you choose, set aside ten minutes *every day*. If you prefer, you may divide the time into two five-minute periods. Either way, make sure you exercise daily. You won't be helping yourself if you skip days and then try to make up the time in half-hour bursts of effort. In only ten minutes a day you are unlikely to have time for more than three of the exercises on the list. But to break the monotony, you might select six exercises you like and alternate them — three one day, another three the next.

Don't rush through any exercise. You're not in a race, and you'll benefit more if you take your time. Repeat the motions of each exercise as often as you think is sensible or until you have filled your ten minutes for the day. There is no harm in doing more than ten minutes, if you feel like it, but don't let it get out of control. I have known many back patients, myself included, to gradually expand the exercise period to thirty minutes or more as they gain strength. Then, when the exercises become too much of a nuisance, they simply stop. Patients don't cut down, they cut out.

Read the instructions carefully and follow them closely. In particular, make sure that your starting position is correct. This is important not only to make the exercise effective but also to avoid needless discomfort. If an exercise does cause pain, don't abandon it without considering first what kind of pain you feel.

Muscular pain may develop from the unaccustomed exercising of neglected muscles. This is no cause for alarm. If possible, put up with the discomfort until the muscles stop complaining. Or, if you prefer, switch to another exercise for a day or two and then go back to the first one when those sore muscles have had a rest.

Aggravation of back pain is not dangerous or harmful in moderate doses, but it may discourage you from exercising. If that's the pain you're feeling, substitute another exercise from the list and see if the problem clears up. If every exercise aggravates your back pain, the trouble may be pressure on a nerve (Type Three pain), or the pain may be originating from outside your spine — from a mild kidney infection, for example. If pain proves to be a problem with every exercise you try, I suggest that you check with your doctor or your physiotherapist.

Neck pain may result from the abdominal exercises. People with weak stomach muscles often strain their neck muscles just trying to do a sit-up. You can avoid this problem by tucking your chin against your chest while doing the abdominal exercises, and by taking up the neck exercises described later in this chapter.

To avoid needless pain in your low back, avoid raising both legs from the floor at the same time while lying on your back. Double straight-leg raising will force you to arch your back unless it is unusually strong, and it is the arching, of course, that causes the pain.

In each exercise, hold the muscles at their maximum contraction for six seconds before relaxing slowly.

Three terms are used to describe the positions in which the abdominal exercises are performed:

Supine means lying on your back with your legs straight.

Crook lying means lying on your back with your hips and knees bent and your feet flat on the floor.

Half-crook lying means lying on your back with one hip and knee bent and one leg straight on the floor.

Easy Exercises

1. THE PELVIC TILT

Application: Types One, Two, or Three. This is among the few exercises suitable for people with Type Three pain.

Starting position: Crook lying.

Exercise: Tighten your abdominal muscles (but do not hold your breath). Now flatten the small of your back against the floor by rolling your hips. Raise your buttocks slightly but do not push with your feet — all the pull should come from your abdominal muscles. Hold for six seconds; relax for six seconds. Then repeat six times.

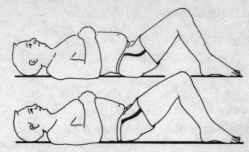

Fig. 15. The Pelvic Tilt is basic to most abdominal strengthening exercises.

Comment: I suggest you practise the pelvic tilt often until you can do it easily and well. It is used as the preparatory contraction before all the other back exercises.

Once you have mastered the pelvic tilt while lying on the floor, you will find it useful to perform the same exercise while standing up, since you need to be able to stand and walk with a pelvic tilt to carry out your activities of daily living.

1a. THE STANDING PELVIC TILT

Application: Types One, Two, or Three.

Starting position: Stand with your back against a wall, placing your feet about six inches away from the baseboard.

Exercise: Tilt your pelvis by pulling in your stomach and squeezing your buttocks gently together. This should flatten your low back against the wall. Keep your shoulders relaxed. Do not hold your breath. Hold this position for six seconds; then relax for six seconds. Repeat this sequence six times.

Comment: Once you have the knack of the standing pelvic tilt, you can do it anywhere, substituting an imaginary wall for the real one.

2. HEAD RAISING

Application: Type One or Type Two.

Starting position: Crook lying. Adopt and hold the pelvic tilt.

Next step: Hold your arms straight up in the air. Tuck your chin against your chest.

Exercise: Lift your head towards your knees, rolling up as if to sit up. Keeping your feet on the floor, raise yourself until your shoulder blades clear the floor. Hold for six seconds, recline for six seconds, then repeat six times.

3. LEG RAISING

Application: Type One or Type Two.

Starting position: Half-crook lying.

Next step: Adopt the pelvic tilt and hold it.

Exercise: Keeping the knee of your straight leg tight, raise this leg slowly to the level of the bent knee, then lower it slowly to the floor. Repeat this movement six times with each leg.

4. HEAD AND SHOULDER RAISING

Application: Type One.

Starting position: Crook lying.

Next step: Adopt the pelvic tilt and hold it. Hold your arms parallel in front of you.

Exercise: Lift your head and shoulders and reach with both hands to the right side of your knee. Return to your starting position. Now repeat the movement, this time to the left side of the left knee. Both shoulders must clear the floor each time, so that you lift without rolling. Perform twelve of these movements — six alternately to each side.

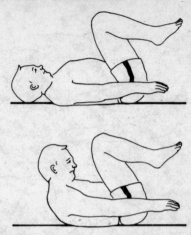

Fig. 16. The Curl puts you in a fetal position while lying on your back.

5. THE CURL

Application: Type One or Type Two.

Starting position: Crook lying.

Next step: Adopt the pelvic tilt and hold it. Bring your knees to your chest. Tuck your chin down onto your chest. Hold your arms straight at your sides and slightly raised.

Exercise: Curl yourself up, aiming your forehead for your knees. Now uncurl — head first, then knees. Repeat six times.

6. CROSS-ARM KNEE PUSHING

Application: Types One, Two, or Three.

Starting position: Crook lying.

Next step: Adopt the pelvic tilt and hold it. Bend your right hip and knee to form a ninety-degree angle. Place

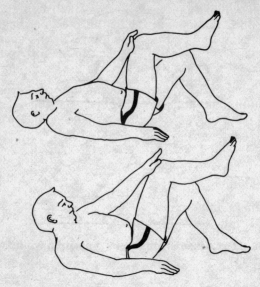

Fig. 17. Cross-Arm Knee Pushing is an isometric exercise; there should be no movement.

your left hand on your right knee and keep your arm straight. Raise your head and tuck in your chin.

Exercise: Push your leg with your arm to create a good abdominal contraction. Count to six. Relax. Repeat this process six times with the same arm and leg. Now change to the other arm and leg and repeat the whole sequence.

Intermediate Exercises

7. ALTERNATE LEG RAISING

Application: Type One or Type Two.

Starting position: Supine.

Next step: Adopt the pelvic tilt and hold it. Keep both legs straight.

Exercise: Raise one leg up, keeping it straight. Raise it only until the knee of the leg on the floor begins to bend. Now lower the leg slowly. Next, repeat the exercise with the other leg. Continue until you have raised each leg six times.

Comment: In this exercise, you must work consciously to maintain that pelvic tilt, because when you are lying flat you tend to arch your back — and lose the tilt to your pelvis.

8. KNEE RAISING

Application: Type One or Type Two.

Starting position: Crook lying.

Next step: Adopt the pelvic tilt and hold it.

Exercise: Raise both knees to your chest and then lower them slowly until both feet are on the floor. Be sure to keep the small of your back flat against the floor as your legs return to the starting position. Repeat six times.

9. DOUBLE LEG RAISING

Application: Type Two.

Starting position: Supine.

Next step: Adopt the pelvic tilt and hold it. Rest your heels on the seat of a chair, keeping your legs straight.

Exercise: Keeping your knees straight, raise both legs up together until you form a ninety-degree angle at your hips. Return to starting point and relax for six seconds. Repeat six times.

Comment: When you have done this often enough for it to be easy, try starting from a lower position — with your heels on a footstool, for instance. But note that this double leg raising is never begun with both heels on the floor. If you can raise both heels from the floor

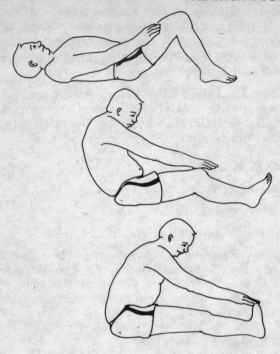

Fig. 18. Toe Touching limits the use of your hip muscles and forces you to use your abdomen. Reaching for your toes stretches the muscles in the backs of your thighs.

without causing pain, your belly muscles are already so strong that you don't need this exercise. Whatever starting point you choose, work consciously to maintain that pelvic tilt.

10. TOE TOUCHING

Application: Type One.

Starting position: Crook lying.

Next step: Adopt the pelvic tilt and hold it. Place your arms on your knees.

Exercise: Straighten your knees gradually as you sit up to reach and touch your toes slowly. Then, as you lower your upper body back to the floor, bend your knees once again. Relax briefly between toe touches and repeat six times.

11. SIT-UP

Application: Type Two.

Starting position: Supine.

Next step: Adopt the pelvic tilt and hold it. With both legs straight, tuck your chin and hold your arms straight up in the air.

Exercise: Try to sit up slowly until your shoulder blades clear the floor. Stop there, count to six, and then lower yourself slowly. Repeat six times.

Comment: This is another exercise where you have to work at maintaining that pelvic tilt. For those unable to do this sit-up, let me suggest a beginner's version called the "sit-down" — which is described right after Exercise 17.

Advanced Exercises

12. LEG RAISING

Application: Type One or Type Two.

Starting position: Supine.

Next step: Adopt the pelvic tilt and hold it.

Exercise: Raise your right leg up straight, raising your upper body at the same time. Now slide your right hand up your leg, aiming for the ankle. Return to your starting position. Now repeat with the left side. Repeat six times on each side.

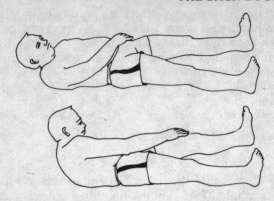

Fig. 19. Because the Oblique Sit-up starts with the legs straight, you must actively maintain the pelvic tilt to avoid arching your back. This exercise strengthens the muscles on the sides of your body and may help to slim your waistline.

13. OBLIQUE SIT-UP

Application: Type One.

Starting position: Supine.

Next step: Adopt the pelvic tilt and hold it. Part your legs, still straight out on the floor. Place your right arm across your body. Tuck in your chin.

Exercise: Try to sit up slowly until your shoulder blades clear the floor, aiming your right shoulder for the left leg. Recover, then repeat, using the opposite arm and leg. Do six of these sit-ups toward each leg.

14. LEG SPREADING — SEATED

Application: Type One or Type Two.

Starting position: Sit on the floor with your legs straight and together and your palms on the floor behind you for support.

Exercise: Bend your knees to your chest, then straighten your legs in mid-air. To the count of six, part your legs, bring them together, and return to rest position.

Comment: If you want to make this exercise even more demanding, extend your arms to the sides at shoulder level and repeat the leg movements.

15. LEG LOWERING

Application: Type Two.

Starting position: Supine.

Next step: Adopt the pelvic tilt and hold it. Bring your knees up to your chest.

Exercise: Lower and straighten one leg slowly until it is almost touching the floor. Now begin to lower the remaining bent leg in the same manner, meanwhile bringing the first leg back up to the bent position at the chest. Repeat this action six times slowly, alternately bending and straightening the legs.

16. LEG SPREADING — SUPINE

Application: Type Two.

Starting position: Supine.

Next step: Adopt the pelvic tilt and hold it. Bend your knees to your chest, straighten them in the air, and then lower them to form an angle of 45 to 60 degrees at your hips. The small of your back must remain on the floor; this will determine the angle at the hips.

Exercise: Spread your legs apart and bring them back together six times, keeping your legs at this level. Now return your knees to your chest, relax, and repeat the sequence.

Comment: This is a modified version of the old exercise favored in training football players. The lower you hold your legs while parting them, the harder it is.

17. THE FULL SIT-UP

Application: Type One or Type Two.

Starting position: Crook lying.

Next step: Adopt the pelvic tilt and hold it. Place your hands behind your head or, if you prefer, your palms against your jaws, with your fingers extending below your ears. Tuck your chin in.

Exercise: Beginning with your head and shoulders, slowly bring your upper body to an upright position. Your feet must remain on the floor. Now return gradually to the starting position. Repeat six times.

Comment: For the energetic young person, here's a tougher version of this exercise: instead of moving your upper body all the way up and down, rise only 60 or 70 degrees, then lower yourself to about 20 degrees from the floor. In other words, don't go fully up or fully down but hover between the two extremes.

Would you like an even tougher exercise? If so, try doing your sit-up while lying on your back with your hips and knees bent and legs up on the seat of an average-height chair with your feet unsupported. Hold your hands as you did for the full sit-up — behind your head or with your palms against your jaws. Now assume the pelvic tilt and do the sit-up.

For people whose abdominal muscles are too weak to do even the easiest sit-up, here's an alternative:

The Sit-down

Application: Types One, Two, or Three.

Starting position: Sit on the floor. Draw your knees up towards your chin and hug them.

Exercise: With your arms supporting the weight of your upper body, lean backwards as far as you can. Now pull yourself up again. Repeat six times, resting between each time.

Comment: As you gain strength in the abdominal muscles, relax that tight grip on your knees, so that your upper body is allowed to move progressively closer to the floor. Gradually, after several sessions of this exercise, you should find that you can return to the upright position without using your arms. By then you can abandon the Sit-down for the more conventional Sit-up.

Neck-Strengthening Exercises

Here are four exercises you can do almost anywhere at any time. These are isometric exercises, which means they produce muscle tension without a change in length — "iso" means "equal." In other words, there is no movement, just a tightening of the muscle. Charles Atlas created a body-building empire with exercises of this kind, which he called "dynamic tension."

18. THE BACKWARD PRESS

Starting position: Clasp the fingers of your two hands fully together and place them against the back of your head.

Exercise: Press your head back against your hands and hold the pressure for twelve seconds. Now rest and repeat the action six times.

Comment: Be careful not to push so hard that you cause your neck to quiver, since this will irritate the facet joints in your neck and may cause pain. Just push as hard as you can without causing any movement. This caution applies to all the neck exercises described here.

19. THE FORWARD PRESS

Starting position: Place your palms against your forehead so as to be able to exert a strong pressure.

Exercise: Press your head hard against your hands and hold the pressure for twelve seconds. Rest and then repeat six times.

20. THE RIGHT-SIDE PRESS

Starting position: Cup your right hand against the right side of your head.

Exercise: Press your head hard against your hand and hold the pressure for twelve seconds. Relax for six seconds and then repeat. Do six right presses before moving on to the left-side press.

21. THE LEFT-SIDE PRESS

Perform the same action as the right-side press, using your left hand on the left side of your head.

Neck-Relaxation Exercises

Relaxing your shoulders is a key factor in reducing strain on your neck. Try these three simple methods.

22. THE SHRUG

Shrug your shoulders as high as you can, hold them in this position for six seconds, then let go.

23. THE BACKWARD THRUST

Thrust your shoulders as far back as you can, as though forcing your shoulder blades to meet. Hold this position for six seconds, then let go.

24. THE FORWARD THRUST

Push your shoulders forward as far as you can. Hold this position for six seconds then let go.

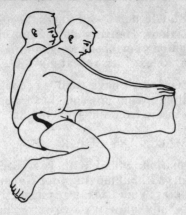

Fig. 20. The Hurdle Stretch.

Thigh Exercises

25. THE HURDLE STRETCH

Starting position: Sit on the floor with one leg bent to the side, the other straight out in front of you. From the inside of the knee to the foot, the bent leg should be touching the floor.

Exercise: With both hands, touch the toes of the extended leg. Repeat. Now reverse the position of your legs and touch the toes of the other foot. Repeat. Do this exercise six times.

Comment: Many doctors believe that tightness in the back of the thigh — the hamstring muscles — produces a swayback posture. This exercise will stretch the muscles in the backs of your thighs, so that you can more readily straighten your lumbar spine. If the toe-touching hurts or is too strenuous for you, just sit in the starting position for a few seconds and then work gradually on the toe-touching.

26. THE HALF-KNEE BEND

Starting position: Stand erect, hands on hips.

Exercise: Slowly bend your knees, keeping your feet flat on the floor. Halfway down, stop momentarily. Now straighten your knees slowly until you are fully erect again. Relax, then repeat six times.

Comment: Once you have tried this one, nobody will have to tell you what muscles it exercises: you'll feel the effects in the fronts of your thighs.

27. THE IMAGINARY CHAIR

Starting position: Stand with your back close to a smooth wall. Without moving your feet any more than necessary, press your back firmly against the wall and slide your body slowly downwards until you are positioned as if seated in a chair, with your thighs parallel to the floor.

Exercise: Hold this position as long as you can. Don't press with your hands on the top of your knees. That makes the exercise easier, and that's cheating.

Comment: Most people who have never tried the Imaginary Chair find it hard to hold for thirty seconds. Don't despair; just do what you can, relax, and repeat. After some days or weeks you will work your way up to a respectable period. Three minutes is considered an achievement by most fit people; in training, Olympic skiers are expected to manage five minutes or more.

You may have noticed that so far I have not asked you to do a full sit-up with your legs out straight or with your feet tucked under the edge of a sofa or a dresser. There is an important reason why. Any sit-up that is done with the legs straight or held down is an exercise *not* for the abdominal muscles but for the hip flexor muscles. Many doctors believe that over-strengthening these hip muscles can contribute indirectly to back pain. When the sit-up is performed from the crook-lying position, the function of the hip flexors is decreased by seventy percent. When the sit-up is done while lying on the back with the hips and knees bent and the legs up on the seat of a chair, the hip muscles are completely inactive, and all the action comes from the abdominal muscles. That is why you may notice that if you are accustomed to doing sit-ups with your legs extended, you will have considerable difficulty at first doing a sit-up while crook-lying. The bent-knee position causes you to make full use of your abdominal muscles, perhaps for the first time in your life.

Occasionally I will find patients who fail to respond to abdomen-strengthening exercises. These are often people who have had back surgery or who suffer from Type Two back pain. In these cases, I will suggest a program of back-arching, commonly known as extension exercises. Let me explain two points about these. First, exercises that arch the back are, generally speaking, more likely to cause back pain than exercises that strengthen the abdomen, particularly if you suffer from Type One back trouble. For this reason, I don't recommend arching exercises for Type One back conditions. Second, if you have been told in the past to try flexion (forward-bending) exercises and are told later to try arching exercises, don't jump to the conclusion that your doctor or therapist is experimenting without really knowing what you need. As with so many other factors affecting back pain, there are no absolutes: it is simply a matter of starting with the program most likely to succeed and then, if it fails, switching to an alternative.

Here, then, are some simple extension (arching) exercises:

Easy Exercises

28. PASSIVE PUSH-UPS

Application: Type Two.

Starting position: Lie flat on your stomach on the floor. If this is uncomfortable, place a small pillow under your stomach. Place your palms flat on the floor just under your shoulders.

Exercise: Keeping your chin tucked in on your chest, press on your hands and lift your head, shoulders, and chest off the floor until your elbows and chest are straight, if possible. Your pelvis remains on the floor. If you begin to feel discomfort in your low back, do not go any higher. Hold to a count of six. Now lower yourself slowly to the floor. Relax for six seconds. Repeat six times.

29. HIP EXTENSION

Application: Type Two.

Starting position: Lie on your stomach over a pillow with your arms by your sides. Bend one knee to a right angle.

Exercise: Keeping your knee bent, lift your thigh just off the floor and hold for six seconds. Lower your thigh to the floor. Relax for six seconds. Repeat with the other leg. Alternate six times on each side.

Comment: Do not lift high enough to cause your low back to arch.

30. ARM EXTENSION

Application: Type Two.

Starting position: Lie on your stomach over a pillow with your arms straight out on the floor above your head.

Exercise: Lift one arm just off the floor and hold for six seconds. Lower your arm to the floor. Relax for six seconds. Repeat with the other arm. Repeat this sequence, six times on each side.

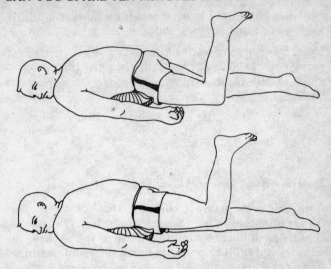

Fig. 21. Hip Extension. Lying over a pillow prevents excessive arching of the low back. Done properly, extension exercises should strengthen the back muscles without increasing pain.

Advanced Exercises

31. HIP EXTENSION — ADVANCED

Application: Type Two.

Starting position: Lie on your stomach over a pillow, with your arms by your sides.

Exercise: Without arching your back, and keeping your knees straight, lift one leg until your thigh is clear of the floor. Hold for six seconds, then lower slowly. Repeat with the other leg. Repeat this sequence six times.

32. TRUNK EXTENSION

Application: Type Two.

Starting position: Lie on your stomach over a pillow, with your arms by your sides.

Exercise: Keeping your chin tucked in on your chest, raise your head and chest slowly until they are just clear of the floor. Lower slowly. Relax. Repeat six times.

Comment: Do not lift high enough to cause your back to arch.

Exercise Routines You Can Try

Here are some sample routines that may suit you. Please note that these are only suggestions to give you some idea of how you might choose to spend those ten minutes a day. It is possible that a different combination of exercises will suit you better. Feel free to create any combination you like.

Remember, too, that there is no need for you to progress from easy exercises to more advanced ones; all you need to do is find a combination you like and stay with them.

As you will notice, the categories I have set out for these routines make no distinction as to gender. There is no need to: except during pregnancy and the postpartum period, women have the same needs and capabilities as men.

The Basic Routine

For Type One
No. 1. The Pelvic Tilt
No. 4. Head and Shoulder
   Raising
No. 17. The Full Sit-up

For Type Two
No. 1. The Pelvic Tilt
No. 5. The Curl
No. 17. The Full Sit-up

The Senior Citizen's Routine

For Type One
No. 1. The Pelvic Tilt
No. 2. Head Raising
No. 6. Cross-Arm Knee
  Pushing

For Type Two
No. 1. The Pelvic Tilt
No. 6. Cross-Arm Knee
  Pushing
No. 8. Knee Raising

The Fitness Buff's Routine

For Type One
No. 12. Leg Raising
No. 13. Oblique Sit-up
No. 14. Leg-Spreading
  — Seated
No. 17. The Full Sit-up
  (legs on chair)

For Type Two
No. 15. Leg Lowering
No. 16. Leg Spreading
  — Supine
No. 17. The Full Sit-up
  (legs on chair)
No. 32. Trunk Extension

The Pregnancy Routine

For Type One
No. 1. The Pelvic Tilt
No. 3. Leg Raising
No. 6. Cross-Arm Knee
  Pushing

For Type Two
No. 1. The Pelvic Tilt
No. 3. Leg Raising
No. 6. Cross-Arm Knee
  Pushing

The Post-Partum Routine

For Type One
No. 1. The Pelvic Tilt
No. 5. The Curl
No. 10. Toe Touching
No. 26. The Half-Knee
  Bend

For Type Two
No. 1. The Pelvic Tilt
No. 5. The Curl
No. 11. The Sit-up
No. 26. The Half-Knee
  Bend

The Limited Routine

For Type One and Type   No. 6. Cross-Arm Knee
   Two   Pushing
No. 1. The Pelvic Tilt

One final word on exercise. Important though it is, your routine of back exercise is not the entire long-term solution to your back problem. It would be unrealistic to expect ten minutes of daily exercise to provide you with control of your symptoms throughout the other twenty-three hours and fifty minutes of each day. Exercise is just one part of a control program that must also include techniques for handling your back during all your activities of daily living (ADL). Although the importance of this aspect of your program may not be as obvious as the importance of exercise, it is equally significant.

But before we move on to the business of long-term control of your back, we must face the immediate problem of coping with your next acute attack.

12 Be Ready for That Next Attack

Nothing will boost your morale and build your self-confidence faster than knowing how to cope with a sudden attack of back pain. As you have probably discovered the hard way, an acute attack can be triggered by the most trivial, routine action — reaching up to a shelf, opening a window, or bending over to put on your shoes. In fact, the action may be so familiar that you cannot even identify it as the movement that triggered your attack. It is important to realize that the triggering incident does not damage your back; it simply activates the source of your pain. In any case, you would find it impossible to avoid all actions and situations that are potential "triggers." The solution, instead, is to be so well informed and prepared that you can deal calmly with an attack from the moment it begins. In that frame of mind, you can avoid the panic that causes your system to tighten up and aggravate your condition.

Typically an attack is signaled by a sudden stab of pain followed rapidly by a muscle spasm. After that, the two may interact repeatedly. The strategy, then, is to take protective action so promptly that the initial pain is eased and the spasm never occurs.

Five Basic Defensive Positions

At the first sign of an attack, lie down as soon as possible and assume a fetal position, either on your back or on one side: knees bent up to your chest and chin tucked well down. The main object is to get out of an upright position so that gravity is no longer creating a load on your spine, and to rotate your pelvis to eliminate extra stress in your low back.

Some back patients prefer other positions that achieve the same effect.

My own favorite position during an attack is to lie on my back on the floor with my legs on top of a chair seat or over the edge of my bed. I use two large pillows, one under my head, the other under my buttocks, and I move my trunk as far under the chair as I can, so that my knees are bent towards my chest. This is almost the same as the fetal position but it works even better for me. Once safe in this position, I stay free of pain.

Another position I use often involves hugging one knee as tightly to my chest as I can. This is done preferably while lying down, but if you can't lie down, you can sit with your back in a corner to provide good spinal support. A pillow behind the back is useful.

The squat is another good position to assume. I use it a lot myself, especially if I am taking a short break between stints in the operating room. It's a helpful way to reduce the tension on the spine for a few minutes and thereby ward off an attack. The squat has one drawback, though: once you're into it, you may find you need somebody to help you stand up again. If you are not an experienced squatter, squat with your back to a wall; otherwise, you will tip over. In fact you may want to use the wall as a means of assuming the squat as painlessly and safely as possible: stand with your back against the wall, then bend your knees and slide down until you have reached a full squat.

Some patients find relief in what might be called "the double leg-hug." They sit down on the floor and hug both legs to the chest. This is really just a variation of the squat, with the body's weight on the buttocks instead of on the feet.

All these alternatives achieve the same basic effects:

Fig. 22. A favorite defensive position.

they unload the spine, flex the pelvis, and provide good abdominal support.

If you have an attack when your choice of positions is limited by practical or social considerations, you may have to compromise a little.

At your desk in the office, for instance, try drawing one leg up to your chest and resting the heel of that foot on the seat of your chair, or on a windowsill. If you have a tilting chair, you may be able to tilt back and push one foot or both against the edge of your desk — a sort of White Collar Fetal Position.

If you are behind the wheel of your car when your back starts to tighten up, you can consider several options, depending on the circumstances. If you are cruising on the highway or driving anywhere in a car without a clutch, you can probably manage to bend your left leg until your left foot is up on the seat. If you are able to pull off the road and stop, you may be able to get out and squat beside the car until the attack begins to subside.

On an aircraft, you can use your seatbelt to good advantage: cinch it tightly to provide good abdominal support, after propping two pillows behind your lower back and supporting your feet on a piece of hand luggage, so that your knees are higher than your hips.

If an attack occurs when you are standing and you can't get off your feet, at least do the pelvic tilt and, if possible, put one foot up on a rail or a curb or anything else that's handy. These two maneuvers help to relax the spinal muscles and avoid the natural tendency all of us have to allow our bellies to sag while we are standing.

If you have found, during a previous attack, that some particular position provides you with better pain relief, use it. Don't feel bound by the suggestions you see here. They are the positions that help most people, but you may be different. It's up to you to find the best way of coping with your back pain.

Your strategy should be entirely defensive. This is no time to go on the offense and experiment with ways of trying to relieve your pain by twisting your back or adopting untried positions. If you have developed a special trick of manipulation that works for you, that's fine; otherwise, don't try to get lucky by swiveling your hips or performing other active movements you hope will "unlock" your seizure or work it out. Such attempts are unlikely to succeed, and they may hurt or frighten you, thereby aggravating the intensity of your attack. Your best bet is to rely on immobility and rest, after you have assumed the position that provides the most relief.

If you're unlucky enough to have a cold coming on while your back is sore, try to remember this four-line jingle:

> To save your back
> When you cough or sneeze,
> Do the pelvic tilt
> As you bend your knees.

Even the best preventive measures are not foolproof. Sometimes an attack will occur and persist despite your best efforts. When that happens, try to keep one point in mind: no attack is a total setback. The exercises you have done and the good postural habits you have assumed will count for something sooner or later. Even if the new attack produces pain that's as bad as ever, you will likely recover sooner than you did from previous episodes.

The Next Step Is Rest

Once you have done all you can to ward off the attack, follow the cardinal rule for all acute back pain: rest. Get off your feet as soon as possible, make yourself comfortable, and stay put. There is no substitute for rest in a recumbent position to remove the compressive effect of gravity. There is no single correct surface on which you must lie. Some people prefer the floor, others a firm bed, and still others the reclining chair in the TV room. They are all fine, just as long as you are comfortable and your back has a chance to relax. You may need to stay off your feet for as long as a week, but if your program of conservative management is well advanced, you may be up and around again in just a few days. Your recovery also depends on the severity of the attack and the condition of your back. It's just like a broken bone rested in a cast — you have to give it time to heal.

Avoid the urge to "do something" to help your back improve more quickly. After all, you wouldn't break open the cast on a fractured leg every couple of weeks just to see how well it was mending. You would leave it alone until you felt sure it had mended itself sufficiently. Do the same with your back. Make it a firm rule to discontinue all exercises until the pain has subsided considerably. This temporary ban on exercise is not to prevent you from harming yourself — that wouldn't happen — but to prevent you from becoming discouraged by exercises that cause pain. Sometimes people keep exercising during an attack, apparently believing that martyrdom is good for the spine. As a result, they become so disenchanted with the whole program that they simply give up. I hope you won't make that mistake. You will find that there are some substitute exercises that can be carried on even while you are still confined to bed with your attack of pain. You might try belly-tightening, for instance — tightening and relaxing the muscles of your abdomen, which you would otherwise be strengthening by means of other exercises on our list. This is a good way to maintain your daily exercise habit without causing pain.

If you find yourself in a situation where you are unable to rest for long, you may want to try one or more of the remedies described in Chapter Nine. Or, if you have already discovered a remedy that augments the relief you get from resting, by all means use it.

There is no harm, for instance, in taking a pain-reliever, but I don't recommend narcotics. In the proper treatment of back pain there is little place for the use of such drugs. Back problems may become chronic, and if narcotics are used regularly, we face the specter of addiction. Stay with over-the-counter pain-relievers, such as aspirin. If your doctor prescribes some stronger medicine, use it only as directed.

Counter-irritants, on the other hand, are remedies where the choice is entirely yours. If a cold pack or a heating pad helps relieve your pain, indulge yourself. A hot bath and a hot toddy can work wonders.

Anti-inflammatory drugs are no substitutes for rest. Their effects are unpredictable. If you are among those who have success with them, use them. But don't build your personal recovery program around them.

Tranquilizers such as diazepam may help you in some instances, but not if you need to keep your mind alert, or if you happen to be a person who becomes agitated when you are unable to think clearly. Fear and panic are among every back patient's potential enemies, and whether they originate with a drug or arise from a lack of self-confidence, they can trigger a spasm that may prolong your pain needlessly.

Back braces and corsets are especially useful to people whose jobs or other obligations require them to carry on with little or no rest during an attack. The best device of this kind, in my opinion, is a lightweight elastic corset, which encloses your lower trunk like a giant rubber band. Men and women alike can obtain considerable comfort from such appliances, but they should be used only as a temporary means of relief. A good therapeutic corset doesn't actually help your back directly, but its overall body support has a comforting effect that is beneficial even to people whose belly muscles are strong.

Once again I must emphasize that there are no "bests" or absolutes for everyone. There are just two basic principles to remember:

1. Use whatever remedy feels good or seems to work best for you.
2. As long as the pain persists, avoid exercise.

Once your acute attack has subsided — and every acute attack does subside — you will want to get on with the task of maintaining long-term control and going about the business of preventing an acute episode from ever happening again.

13 Living With Your Back

It would be possible to list dozens of rules for avoiding backache during your activities of daily living — your ADL — but, as you realize by now, I am not inclined towards rule-making, either for my readers or for my back patients. I have always found it more practical to stress the right attitude by setting out general principles and then illustrating them with examples.

First, three essentials, in principle:

1. Maintain that pelvic tilt, or as close to it as circumstances allow, throughout virtually every activity. Often, this just means avoid arching your back.
2. When lifting objects, make your legs do the work by squatting or knee-bending. Your back is not a crane.
3. Find ways to assist your spine by improving the mechanical advantage. For example, don't pick up a heavy object at arm's length if you can hug it against your body.

Now let's see how these principles can be applied to various activities.

Night Rest

You can maintain your best pelvic position by lying on your back with a small pillow under your head and your legs kept in a moderate crook position. As you may have discovered, solid foam pillows are hard on your neck, so if you have neck pain along with back trouble, use a pillow filled with feathers, down, or soft foam chips. Support your knees by rolling three pillows or equivalent material into the shape of a bolster and wrapping them in a blanket, sheet, or sleeping bag. The roll keeps the contents from sagging or displacing during the night. One alternative: raise your lower legs to a horizontal position by supporting them with two soft cushions and a pillow — if you can find a way of keeping them in place all night. If you prefer to sleep on your side, curl into a ball and place a pillow between your knees to prevent your pelvis from rotating. Many people find it more comfortable to draw up only the top leg. Whichever position you use, keep the pillow between your thighs.

Sleeping on your stomach often leads to morning backache. If you can break the habit, do so. If not, try sleeping with a pillow under the front of your pelvis to reduce the sag in your low back. For nights when your back just won't get comfortable, I suggest you try a variation of one of the five defensive positions described in Chapter Twelve. Put a seat cushion on the floor, pillows under your head and buttocks, and your lower legs and feet up on the bed. Get as close to the bed as you can and pull the covers down over you. I have used this position to get to sleep when my back was particularly sore. Usually when I awake in the middle of the night my feet are cold but my back feels better, and I can climb into bed again. One patient of mine keeps a sleeping bag under her bed with her so that she doesn't even have to get up.

Day Rest

Here are three positions favored by most back patients, especially when recovering from a pain attack.

Position 1: For reading or watching television while lying down, lie on the floor on your back with your legs in a crook position. Place a fairly thick pillow under your head and a slim pillow under your buttocks, to keep your pelvis tilted properly. If the floor seems too hard, use a chaise longue cushion, or similar long pad, as a mattress.

Position 2: Arrange your upper body as in Position 1

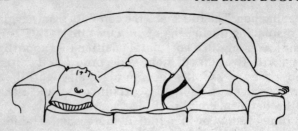

Fig. 23. Resting positions unload the low back by eliminating gravity and excess curvature.

and place your lower legs across a chair seat or coffee table cushioned to suit your comfort. I am sure that this position has saved me from a severe attack of back pain on at least one occasion. I was carrying a heavy armload of firewood into the house when I lost my footing on the doorstep. In an effort to keep from falling, I twisted my back and felt something happen — I'm sure you know the feeling. Fortunately, it was a Sunday afternoon and there was a good football game on television, and so I took to the living-room floor, watched the game, and remained in this position for several hours. The attack I anticipated never developed.

Position 3: Lie on your back on a sofa and assume a modified crook position by placing your feet flat on one of the sofa's arms. You'll want at least one pillow under your head.

Sitting

Most people don't realize that sitting is hard on your back. As you may recall from my comments in Chapter Three, there is a greater load on the discs in your spine when you are in a sitting position, especially if you are bending forward, than when you are standing erect. This is one reason why many people with desk jobs complain of back pain.

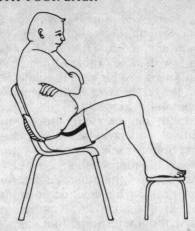

Fig. 24. Comfortable sitting often resembles a controlled slump. Even a good sitting posture may become uncomfortable, so change your position frequently.

Start with a comfortable chair — well padded but not overstuffed. It should have a firm back that slopes backward about ten degrees and a seat that supports your thighs slightly above the level of your hips. Rocking chairs and recliners are great, but they do make desk work difficult.

If you are concerned about choosing an office or work chair, your best choice is a tilter that also locks upright. With it, you can either lock it to gain support for your lumbar spine, or release it to allow you to tilt back and relax. Also, make sure it treats your legs right: the front of the seat shouldn't cut into the backs of your legs, and ideally it should have a footrest enabling you to keep your knees higher than your hips. If there is no footrest, use a separate footstool or equivalent. Whatever arrangement you have, change your position frequently, to rest those muscles and joints.

Here are five comfortable solutions to the problem of sitting with a bad back.

Position 1: First, a comfortable way to slump. Place your hips forward on the seat of a chair and your feet flat on the surface of a footstool. Put a pillow or pad behind your low back to prevent it from sagging, and be sure your knees are higher than your hips.

Position 2: Sit on the floor with your back against a wall and hug your knees.

Position 3: Sit on the floor, cross-legged, in the Indian tradition. This pose leaves your hands free.

Position 4: Slump back in a chair — that is, with shoulders back, hips forward, and the calf of one leg resting on the knee of the other. Again, remember to support your back with a cushion or pillow.

Position 5: If a seat is low enough, you can be comfortable without additional foot support because your knees will be high enough with your feet on the floor. Passenger seats in some cars provide comfort in this way, but extra low-back support with a car cushion is often useful.

You probably realize by now that these five positions have one thing in common: they all require you to assume a pelvic tilt.

One of the best opportunities for planning your sitting to protect your back arises every time you travel on an airplane. Carry a piece of hand luggage to put under the seat ahead, where it can act as a footstool. Ask a flight attendant for two pillows and put them both behind the small of your back. Always select an aisle seat so that you can easily get up and stretch every half-hour or so. Even long flights should present no problems if you follow these simple suggestions.

Home Duties — Sitting

Again, observe the principle of the pelvic tilt — knees higher than hips — and you can't go far wrong. In the kitchen, keep utensils within easy reach. Where a low chair won't do, use a high stool with a high step or rung for your feet. Arrange your seating so that counter tops or other work surfaces are two inches below your elbows. When reading, support your arms on a table or desk.

Home Duties — Standing

Never stand flat-footed if you can put one foot up on a stool or a low shelf — the posture drinkers assume at a stand-up bar. Saloon keepers discovered the comfort of this position long before doctors developed the theory behind it, and there's no reason why you can't enjoy its advantages in your own home. It is just another way of maintaining the pelvic tilt.

During activities that may aggravate your pain — painting high places, cleaning overhead shelves — rotate your activities to avoid prolonged strain. Rest often, if only for a few moments each time.

Sweeping the floor, vacuuming a carpet, and raking leaves can all cause pain by excessive movement of your low back. The proper way to carry out these tasks is to use your legs, lunging like a fencer while keeping your back as immobile as possible. It may sound silly, but with practice it can be done so easily that nobody will notice, and your back will feel so much better.

Work Surfaces

For most people with back trouble, the ideal height for a work surface, such as a desk, counter, or table top, is two inches below the elbow. Since most work surfaces are non-adjustable, you should try to overcome any discrepancy by providing an item of the right height for sitting or standing, such as a stool to sit on if the surface is too low for standing comfortably. Also, keep in mind that a work surface of ideal height ceases to be ideal if you are working on an object that is tall or bulky. For example, if you try to repair a chair on top of a work bench, the operation may be too high for comfort.

Office Duties

You can do your back a great favor with a device as simple as a fat telephone directory placed under your feet while you're seated at your desk.

Shift around often. Pull open a low desk drawer and use it for a footstool while you chat with a visitor or talk on the phone. Cross your knees often — that raises at least one knee above hip level. If you're the boss, put your feet up on the desk.

Avoid That Arch

Reaching up to overhead shelves, opening double-hung windows, strap-hanging in buses and subway trains — these are all movements that cause back pain by forcing your spine to arch. Holding a pelvic tilt may reduce the height of your reach a little, but it is one way to avoid backache. When the arch in the back is pronounced and habitual, it's called lordosis — according to one medical legend, named for the way the imperious lords of old arched their spines as they sat in the saddle, haughtily staring down at lesser mortals. It's a shame the peasants never knew what a price their masters were paying in backache for assuming that arrogant pose.

Squat and Give Your Spine a Rest

Squatting is the ideal way of resting your spine. In cultures where it's customary to squat, common backache is almost unknown. If the traditional East Indian squat doesn't sit well with your leg muscles and joints, compromise by going down on one knee with the other foot flat on the floor. Try to squat in any situation where you might otherwise kneel fully or bend at the waist. The squat is ideal for tending your garden, hobnobbing with small children, or socializing at informal parties where some guests sprawl on the floor.

Lifting

There is no single right way to lift an object. The right way in a given situation will depend on the size and weight of the load and the conditions under which it is to be lifted, such as the access you have to it. The three basic principles are:

1. Take advantage of mechanical leverage by keeping the burden as close as possible to your body.
2. Do as much of the lifting and turning as you can with leg muscles, rather than back muscles.
3. Keep your back erect and balanced. This is not the same as making it ramrod straight; some lifts require you to tilt your upper body forward, in which case you should make your hips do the bending, not your spine.

Body weight, momentum, and even gravity can be used to your advantage. The method you choose may combine these principles and forces in various ways. To lift a heavy carton from the floor, for instance, I would crouch close to it, hug it to my chest, and then rise by straightening my legs. This style of lift is good for my back but it does place quite a strain on my knees. To lug a heavy tool chest from a high shelf and move it across the room, I would rely on gravity, momentum, and my own agility, pulling the box off the shelf and using gravity to create a momentum with which I would spin on the balls of my feet so as to move in the desired direction and carry the box, all in one continuous motion. This is one example of many lifting situations where you may be inclined to rotate your spine — a motion that is bad for any sore back.

When you have to turn while lifting, avoid spinal rotation by turning your feet instead. The best lift is whatever you find, in the circumstances, to be safe, comfortable, and effective.

The most hazardous lifts are the ones for which you are unprepared. For example, you and a companion may be carrying a heavy chest of drawers up a staircase when he stumbles, shifting the whole load to you unexpectedly. This leaves you no time to brace yourself and protect your spine. Before you get into a situation like that, discuss the lift until you both agree on how you will provide yourselves with maximum protection in the event of a mishap. Then make sure you adopt a lifting technique that gives you maximum mechanical advantage. Use these precautions even for lifting tasks that don't seem particularly onerous.

The most difficult lift — even when you are prepared for it — is one where a heavy object must be raised at arm's length and then hoisted over a sash or barrier. One familiar example is the problem of removing an outboard motor from the trunk of a car. Another is the task of lifting a forty-pound child out of a high-sided crib or playpen.

The solution is to avoid lifting from a distance and to deal with the barrier by minimizing its effect on your task. When reaching for the outboard motor, for instance, put one foot either on the bumper or, better still, right inside the car trunk. This places your body as close as possible to the burden before the lift begins. In the nursery, let the side of the crib down — if it's that kind of design — and then bend your knees as much as necessary to clasp the child close to your chest. You can save some strain if you teach the child to come to you and stand up to be lifted.

No matter how shrewd you are about sparing your back, there will be times when you simply can't avoid using and perhaps straining those spinal muscles and joints. And that is exactly why those conditioning exercises are so important: they provide you with that reserve in your "back account" so that those unavoidable "withdrawals" can be made without needless pain.

Sexual Intercourse

Like the time-honored headache at bedtime, a backache can become a convenient excuse for avoiding sexual encounters. Because no one can prove you don't have back pain, your excuse for abstinence cannot be challenged successfully. Often, however, sexual frustration and upset marriages are by-products of genuine back trouble because one partner is fearful of triggering an attack of pain. Your back problem needn't deprive you of intercourse if you protect yourself from pain in two ways: As a long-term measure, begin at once on the abdominal exercises described earlier. What better incentive could you have for strengthening those belly muscles? And meanwhile arrange with your partner to assume the positions least likely to strain your back. The key to avoiding strain is to make sure you do not arch your back or your neck.

When the woman is the person with the back problem, the man can help her be comfortable if he lies on his back in the crook position and allows her to straddle his pelvis and then lean forward so that her torso is horizontal and her face is close to his. She rests her elbows above or beside his shoulders to support some of her body weight. In this position, as long as her trunk is well forward, she avoids arching either her low back or her neck.

Similar protection of the woman's spine is provided if she sits astride her lover while facing his feet. In this case she does not bend her torso forward into a horizontal position but remains leaning forward at an angle of about forty-five degrees.

Spinal protection for both partners is provided by a variation of the classic "spoon" position. With the couple both lying on the same side and facing in the same direction, as though she were seated on his lap, the woman parts her knees enough for the man to place his knees between her thighs and gain entry.

Both partners can also minimize pain in their low backs and necks by adopting a face-to-face position while lying on their sides. For instance, the man may lie on his right side while the woman lies facing him on her left. He raises his body long enough to allow her to slip her left leg under his body and her right leg over him. Now they come together until she is, in effect, hugging his waist with her thighs. He can now achieve good stability yet free movement by placing his palms on her buttocks while she entwines her arms around his neck. Some couples find it easier to achieve this position by starting out in the position that is commonly regarded as the basic one for intercourse: that is, with the man on top of the woman. Now the woman raises her legs until they are wrapped around his waist. The couple then turn onto their sides.

If you have not tried the positions described here, you may find that a certain amount of experimentation is necessary before you can achieve comfort and satisfaction. If you are the one with the back problem, your partner must be patient and understanding, and you should conduct yourself in such a way as to encourage that attitude. You will find that the extra effort required of both of you will be well worthwhile, for it can immensely improve a couple's sex life and marital relations.

Pregnancy

The effect of pregnancy on back problems is a very common concern. I am frequently consulted by women who want to become pregnant but are fearful of stirring up their chronic back pain. Naturally, they wonder how great the risks are and what to do to reduce them. Unfortunately, I am obliged to tell these women that the effects of pregnancy on backs is unpredictable. I have seen cases where women with a history of chronic back trouble have gone through an entire pregnancy without so much as a twinge of back pain. On the other hand, I have known women who have never had back trouble in their entire lives — until their spines succumbed to the strain of carrying their firstborn.

Fortunately, there are ways of reducing the risks considerably. If you are planning to become pregnant, you would be well advised to condition yourself through back exercises for several months in advance until you achieve the control that minimizes the likelihood of back pain.

If back pain is going to occur during pregnancy, it usually shows up within the first three months, or else not until the full term is almost completed. Back pain associated with pregnancy is usually the product of stress resulting from alterations in the mechanics of the body while it carries the unborn baby. This problem underlines once again the importance of good abdominal control in protecting your spine. If you lose that control through pregnancy or lack of exercise, your back is asked to take on an extra load that may cause pain. When that occurs, proper treatment consists of protecting the back from additional stress and developing good postural habits.

If you attend a prenatal program you will probably notice the similarity between the type of exercise prescribed there and the exercise program outlined in this book. The reason is that good prenatal care, like good back care, requires protection of the back and sound control of the abdominal muscles. Obviously, your established exercise program will need to be modified during pregnancy, and your own doctor is the best source of advice on this matter.

The principles you adopt as a victim of chronic

backache for protecting your back during daily living
will also need modification. For instance, those high-
heeled shoes that don't necessarily cause you back
pain at other times may cause trouble during pregnancy. Again, on questions about daily activities
where the answers are not clear-cut and obvious,
consult your doctor.

One problem many women overlook is the special
risk of back stress during new motherhood, especially,
of course, when the mother has had backache in the
past. Many women succeed in avoiding back pain
throughout their pregnancy, only to succumb during
the first weeks after the baby is born. This is a time
when the new mother is faced with many unaccustomed tasks. Consequently, she is especially vulnerable during the repetitive bending and lifting involved in nursing, bathing, and dressing the baby
and in handling extra laundry.

This activity takes place at the very time when the
mother's abdomen is still in poor condition from the
effects of pregnancy and she has not yet had time to
regain good abdominal control.

If you find yourself in this situation, I suggest that
you pay special attention to the techniques you use in
your daily tasks, so as to give your back every
reasonable protection. You should also embark on a
new program of back exercises as soon as your doctor
gives his permission.

A baby carrier, worn either over the chest or on the
back, is a useful way of avoiding unnecessary stress
on the lower spine. The value of this device is mainly
that it keeps the weight of the baby close to your body
while avoiding the additional strain of lifting the
baby with your arms. Meanwhile, it leaves you free
to concentrate on proper posture and the pelvic tilt.

Yoga

The relaxation techniques taught in yoga can benefit
victims of common backache at any time, even during

an attack, since this discipline helps to avoid or combat muscle spasm.

Some yoga exercises are also recommended; as you may have noticed, several of the exercises described in Chapter Eleven are similar to yoga exercises, and if you prefer the latter there is no reason why you should not use them, except during an attack. I must add one qualification, however: you would be wise to make a distinction between yoga's flexion or forward-bending exercises, which resemble the back exercises I recommend, and its extension or backward-bending exercises, which you may find painful if you have Type One backache — the worn facet joint. And our general guidelines still apply: don't perform any exercise that hurts, but if it feels good, do it.

Sports

People with back problems sometimes avoid taking part in sports, often on the advice of their doctors. In doing so, they deprive themselves unnecessarily of healthy recreation and the pleasure of friendly competition.

Some sports, of course, are a little too vigorous for people wanting to protect their backs. Once you've had an attack of back pain, you're unlikely to spend weekends sky-diving, hang-gliding, boxing, or engaging in such field sports as pole-vaulting, shot-put, or discus.

But that still leaves several dozen possibilities open, and if you are an otherwise healthy person with a liking for athletics, I see no reason why common backache should keep you on the sidelines. Every sport presents some degree of hazard for the participant, whether he or she has back problems or not. You can break a finger playing ping-pong or a thumbnail digging for clams. The trick is to understand the risks presented by the sport of your choice and conduct yourself accordingly.

I want to make it clear that I'm talking about the stresses that occur in each sport when it is played without serious mishaps. I can't help you decide whether you will find a weekend on the ski slopes worth the risk of an abrupt collision with a tree trunk or, for that matter, engulfment by an avalanche. Here we are considering only the effect on your back of the normal actions necessary in each given sport.

Three forms of strain may be imposed on your spine: weight-loading, rotation, and arching. Weight can cause problems when an unaccustomed load compresses your discs and forces your facet joints to rub painfully together. Rotation places strain on your discs, which do not readily tolerate the twisting that pulls at the fibers of their outer shells. Arching hurts because it squeezes your facet joints and places your spine in an extreme position, robbing it of its normal flexibility. In that position, your back can suffer more pain from any blow.

Here is my estimate of how various recreational sports deserve to be rated in terms of these factors. Some sports are listed in more than one category.

Weight-loading sports

Weight-lifting, an obvious candidate here, creates heavy strain on a bad back. Unless you are an experienced competitor, you would be wise to pass up this one. Somewhat less objectionable entries in this category are curling, bowling (especially tenpins), jogging, horseback riding, motor biking, hunting, and fishing.

Jogging may not seem like a weight-loading sport, but the repetitive stress on the facet joints with each step often leads to backache.

The hazards for hunters and fishermen are the heavy game, heavy fish, and heavy equipment, such as canoes and outboard motors, that need toting.

Rotation-causing sports

Squash is probably the most vigorous of these, with racketball a close second and tennis a distant third. Golf, though less lively than the racket sports, imposes a tremendous rotational force on your spine. Avid golfers with back pain may find the need to shorten each game or modify their swing. Soccer involves a lesser element of spinal rotation. Rotation isn't a serious factor in skiing — unless you ski incorrectly. Good skiers turn their legs, not their spines, and they seldom have back problems from rotational action. Baseball (including softball or fastball) could be considered rotational because of the motion involved in batting, but you are only at bat three or four times in a typical game, and the risk of back pain is therefore much less than in, say, golf.

Sports that arch your back

Hockey is guilty of making you arch your back as you hold that stick against the ice. The three favorite net sports — tennis, badminton, and volleyball — all induce arching, at least while you're serving. Basketball, baseball, rowing, canoeing, skiing, archery, and certain swimming styles, especially the breast stroke, are also "arching" sports.

One of the few sports to which I'd give a clean bill of health is cycling, which hunches you over but really induces what you might call a pelvic tilt on wheels.

Your basic strategy in picking a suitable sport should be to understand the risks in each case and make your choices accordingly. And, where feasible, you should modify your actions or techniques to minimize the discomfort. If you're a golfer, don't lug a bagful of clubs around; recruit a caddy or use a cart. On the tennis court, modify that service to reduce the arch in your back. As a jogger, wear the proper shoes and jog on resilient surfaces whenever you can. For some sports, a back brace may give you temporary comfort and protection.

Above all, remember that, apart from the trauma of an accident — which, after all, can happen anywhere to anybody — even the most vigorous sports activities won't harm your back; they may simply make it hurt for a few days. As we've learned repeatedly throughout this book, hurt is not the same as harm, and the trade-off may be worth it to you, in immediate pleasure and in feeling like a normal person instead of a semi-invalid.

Whatever sport you choose, keep in mind that the general fitness it provides is no substitute for those special ten-minute sessions of daily exercise you need. Your personal program of conservative back management will succeed only if you combine its three essential elements: abdominal exercise, proper activities of daily living, and, perhaps most important of all, the attitude of a person who has taken charge of his or her back problem.

14 You Are Not Alone

I hope you have recognized yourself and your symptoms repeatedly in this book. If so, you will have come to realize that as a victim of common backache you have problems that are not unique. Millions of others suffer the same pain as yours and harbor the same concerns and fears about future attacks. I hope you prove to be one of many who find it possible to benefit from the simple advice I have provided.

You may wonder why you never received the same information from your own doctor. From my own experience I know how hard it can be for a doctor to dispense even the most basic information to all the patients who want and need it.

Only too well do I remember one typical example of that difficulty. It occurred just before five o'clock on a busy afternoon. My desk was littered with the day's accumulation of paper: accident reports to be completed, patients' records, neglected correspondence — a full evening's work at the very least. And I was now precisely thirteen minutes late for a meeting with the senior professor of surgery at the university where I teach.

At that moment, however, I felt obliged to push both professor and paperwork into the back of my mind and focus full attention on the patient seated across the desk from me. She was a charming and attractive middle-aged woman who suffered from typical discogenic back pain.

Unfortunately, she was intent on telling me far more

than I had time to hear. This was her first visit to my office, and she felt I should learn everything about her medical background. And so she went on. And on.

I fidgeted in my chair. I glanced at the clock. I pursed my lips as if I were about to utter something terribly profound about her condition. Perhaps that would cue her to stop talking and start listening. Would this medical saga never end?

At last it did. Concluding her narrative, she sat back in her chair and delivered one last, unforgettable comment.

"You know," she said, "I really appreciate this chance to sit and talk to you. The surgeon I used to see was always too busy. I'm so glad you have the time to sit and listen."

At that point I managed a wan smile, but as I saw her to the door, I realized, perhaps better than she did, that I had failed to give her the information she needed to control her back. I had listened but I had not advised. She would be back, and I would have to make time to add practical instruction to my moral support.

That woman's need for an empathetic ear and my increasingly heavy schedule provided the final part of my motivation to organize the groups that have since developed in Canada and abroad as Back Education Units.

As an orthopedic surgeon seeing a parade of sore backs day after day, I had found myself becoming increasingly bored with my own words as I delivered the same basic message to patient after patient. *Treat an acute attack with rest. Then begin exercising. Adopt good habits in your daily activities. Be patient. Persevere. Don't expect a cure, only control. Give your back the chance it needs to get better by itself.* Important and useful advice, and easy enough to dispense. But can you imagine having to say it over and over, a dozen times every day?

Of course there is a better way. Many medical

centers have begun educating back patients in classes, usually groups of just a dozen or so, where participants, unlike my garrulous office visitor, have a ready-made, fully available audience: each other.

The program operated by the Canadian Back Education Units, of which I am director, is typical of the back schools now to be found in many parts of the world.

If you were to enroll in one of our classes, you would be invited to attend a series of four ninety-minute lectures, once a week for four weeks. Your first session would be conducted by an orthopedic surgeon or other musculoskeletal specialist, who would outline the anatomy, physiology, and disorders accounting for common back pain. At the second session, a physiotherapist would describe the basis of physiotherapy and the effectiveness of back care, including the exercises described in Chapter Eleven. A psychiatrist would take over on the third evening, discussing the part that emotion plays in chronic pain and the psychiatric aspects of back trouble — the points I covered in Chapter Six. For the final session you would move out of the lecture room and into an exercise room or gymnasium, where you could stretch out on the floor while a psychologist instructed you in relaxation and a physiotherapist reviewed good posture, with special attention to the pelvic tilt. Ours is not an exercise or fitness class. The purpose of this final session is only to provide a practical demonstration.

If the course made a typical impression on you, you would complete the fourth session with a new appreciation of your back and its problems. Now you would have a good grasp of the basics that are set out in this book.

I'm not saying we win them all. At 5 p.m. one Friday I got a call at my office from a woman who said she had just "failed" the course.

"What are you going to do for me now?" she

demanded. As patiently as I could, I reviewed the
highlights of what she had supposedly learned at the
lectures. And then I threw the responsibility right
back at her. What did she want to do next?

"What I really think will cure me," she said, blatant-
ly ignoring the fundamental principle that nothing
cures common backache, "is hydrotherapy."

Clearly, this woman didn't care to hear about the
steps she would have to take to control her own back
pain. It would not interest her to learn that hydrotherapy simply relieves symptoms temporarily. Since
nothing else would do, I prescribed hydrotherapy for
her — and made a note not to order therapy again or
waste any more of the therapist's time, once that short
program of treatment was finished.

For every person like that woman there are a dozen
who derive great benefit from nothing more than the
opportunity to talk honestly and openly about common backache and its control, even for six short hours
spread over four weeks.

Anyone with an open-minded attitude can achieve
an enormous sense of satisfaction from learning how
to control back pain and from realizing that there is no
longer any need to fear the next attack. And that
satisfaction is somehow heightened when the learning
takes place in a small and friendly group of fellow
patients.

It's often said that misery loves company, but I am
talking about a rapport that's warmer and far more
humane than what the proverb implies. If you suffer
from common backache, it is reassuring, to say the
least, to realize that thousands of people right in your
own community know exactly how you feel, and that
others have absorbed the advice you are getting, have
put it into practice, and have found themselves able to
resume a normal life-style. The interpersonal moral
support that participants provide to each other, almost from the beginning of the first lecture, is compa-

rable to what occurs at a typical meeting of Alcoholics Anonymous.

That support has its practical aspects, too. One of my patients, a tiny woman I'll call Violet Anderson, complained during a visit to my office that she suffered back pain every time she drove her car. The car was an early-model Vega, with the brake and gas pedals set in an extremely recessed position. As she sat at the wheel, tiny Mrs. Anderson was forced to stretch both legs straight out — a position that inevitably arched her back and caused pain. I suggested that she have a mechanic modify the pedals, adding extensions or blocks that would permit her feet to be lower and closer to the car seat. She took my advice, and driving was no longer a painful experience.

Soon after that, she was attending a Back Education lecture when another woman in the class complained of back pain mainly when she drove her Vega.

"It's the gas pedal!" Mrs. Anderson cried, leaping out of her chair and bounding over to give her fellow sufferer the full benefit of her own expertise — where to have the pedals blocked, how much it would cost, even the name of the mechanic. Episodes like that make me believe that back-school students sometimes get almost as much satisfaction out of helping each other as they do out of helping themselves.

When attitudes like that prevail, the group's learning process gathers its own momentum. It's easier to accept and absorb new information and concepts when others around you are doing the same. Our students quickly appreciate that they are not there to learn some cut-and-dried series of exercises by rote, but to understand their own spines and to use and strengthen them according to a set of simple, common-sense principles.

They quickly rid themselves of any notion of magical secrets and instant cures. They happily clear up all their old misconceptions about "slipped discs" and backs that "go out." And they gain a new appreciation of what their own doctors and physiotherapists have tried to do for them. Usually they become better, more co-operative patients than they were before.

In that respect, I hope this book has the same effect on you as our Back Education Units have on most of their participants. I hope you share their realization that you can take charge of your own back and its problems, and that in doing so you will simply be following the example of thousands of other people who had problems exactly like yours.

Since you may never have the opportunity to make that discovery at a back school, I have compiled a list of questions that are often asked during our sessions, along with the answers you might hear.

Question: My doctor prescribed pills for me and I have been taking them. But you hardly ever mention pills. Don't you believe in medicine?

Answer: Certainly I believe in medicine — for people with diseases. But in the strictest sense of the term you do not have a "medical" problem or a disease. You have a sore back that got that way from normal wear and tear. It makes sense to take insulin for diabetes or digitalis for heart disease. Such drugs combat those diseases. But taking aspirin, or something far stronger, does not combat a worn facet or a bulging disc; it merely masks the symptoms. Pain-killing pills are acceptable, over the short term, to deal with an acute attack; and anti-inflammatories and muscle relaxants also have their place in short-term treatment. But they are not curative, and they are not acceptable substitutes for long-term, conservative management of a back problem.

Question: I realize I'm a little overweight. If I reduce, will my sore back get better?

Answer: Probably not, if you simply lose weight without adopting any positive back-care habits. Extra weight is not a basic cause of back pain, but it does create two additional problems: it discourages you from doing the exercises that would help keep your back in shape, and it aggravates the pain caused by wear and tear. The degree of aggravation depends not only on the amount of excess weight but also on your body build and on the strength of your abdominal muscles. The tendency of men to put extra weight onto their mid-sections is especially pronounced.

The fact that obese men tend to have back trouble more readily than thin men was one of several interesting findings that came out of a study we made of over three thousand patients in our Back Education Units — a large sample for a study of this kind.

Some of the other findings, in brief:

— Obese men with back problems tend to become even heavier as they grow older, while female back patients tend to become thinner.

— Tall people more often have back problems than short people.

— There are two periods in our lives when we are most vulnerable to common backache: first, between the ages of thirty-five and forty-five, and, second, between fifty-five and fifty-nine.

— Women in their late fifties are the most vulnerable group of all.

Question: A few weeks ago I strained by back lifting a bag of groceries out of the trunk of my car. My back has bothered me ever since. What about accidents that cause this kind of back pain?

Answer: Major accidents are an obvious cause of back pain. People who sustain fractures of the spine will inevitably suffer, at least temporarily. But that is not the kind of accident that commonly triggers pain from normal wear and tear. About half the people who develop symptoms from a worn disc or joint relate the onset of their pain to some minor accident. In reality, however, their mishaps have nothing to do with causing or accelerating the natural aging process, although the trauma may make the process painful for the first time.

To illustrate this point, I often use the analogy of the motorist driving a car with a worn tire. The car drives over a pothole and the tire blows out. What caused the blowout? If the tire had been new, it would have gone through the pothole without difficulty. If the worn tire had missed the pothole, it would have been good for another five thousand miles. Obviously, the blowout was caused by a combination of two factors — a degree of natural wear, plus a precipitating episode.

Question: I believe my back pain resulted from a pulled muscle, but my doctor told me I had a "myofascial sprain." You haven't said anything about that.

Answer: Muscle sprains do occur in the back, but they aren't common. Your back has a powerful group of small muscles that are well designed to protect themselves against damage. A significant injury, however, can damage a portion of the muscles in your back, just as a kick in the thigh can cause a charley horse. But it doesn't happen often, and it's not the kind of thing you experience without noticing it at the time. "Chronic" back muscle sprain is usually just a way of describing a muscle spasm that accompanies the wear and tear of Type One or Type Two back pain, and I've certainly said something about that. Generally, a "pulled muscle" is the result, not the cause, of the problem, and treating only the muscle pain misses the underlying condition, which can lead to more trouble in the future.

Incidentally, "myofascial" means "relating to mus-

cles and fibrous tissue." "Myofascial sprain" is just
Doctor for a pulled muscle.

Question: You say that exercise is good for a bad back,
but my doctor tells me to stay in bed. Who's right?

Answer: It's a question of timing. With any acute
attack of back pain, the first thing you need is bed rest.
When that has helped relieve the pain, you can start
thinking about easing gently into an exercise routine.

Question: Should I wear a back brace? If so, for how
long?

Answer: Use your back brace as you would a pair of
work gloves — as something to be put on for a special
purpose, then removed when the job is done. You wear
work gloves when you dig in the garden, but not when
you sit down to eat breakfast. If a back brace gives you
a feeling of abdominal support and confidence during
certain activities, by all means wear it. But take it off
when the situation no longer demands it. And try to
strengthen your abdomen so that the brace becomes
increasingly unnecessary.

Question: If I have a pinched nerve, can the nerve still
function?

Answer: Yes, usually. Type Three back pain does not
ordinarily prevent the affected nerve from functioning. Loss of normal nerve function, seen as genuine
weakness in certain muscle groups or as an absent
reflex, is rare in Type Three pain, and, remember,
Type Three is the least common of the major causes of
back pain.

Question: My exercises hurt. What's wrong? Should I
keep them up?

Answer: If an exercise hurts, don't do it. It won't harm

you, but why suffer needless pain? Work on the principle that anything that feels bad is to be avoided — unless it provides compensating benefits that constitute a worthwhile trade-off. Apply this principle to exercise, recreational sports, and any other activities that are optional.

Question: My doctor has told me I shouldn't wear high-heeled shoes because they are bad for my back. What do you think?

Answer: No doubt about it — shoes with very high heels alter your normal posture, forcing you to arch your back in order to stand erect. As you know by now, arching your back is one of the commonest ways of causing back pain. It's important to realize that, as with so many other activities, arching does not harm your back, even though it causes discomfort or pain. So what it comes down to is this: each time you wear high heels you are making another withdrawal from your "back account." If you are willing to accept backache as a consequence of wearing high heels, then my advice is to go ahead.

Incidentally, it isn't your back that takes the real punishment. Your body is so well designed that the effect of high-heeled shoes is dissipated first through your ankles, then through your knees and your hips, so that little of it reaches your back. In other words, high-heeled shoes put far greater stress on the bones of your feet and the muscles of your legs than on your spine.

Question: Are you sure physiotherapy is a good idea? I tried it once and it didn't help me a bit.

Answer: That's like saying you don't believe in "medicine" because you had some once and it didn't help you. There are many forms of treatment that fall under the heading of physiotherapy — hot packs, ultrasound, electrical stimulation, massage, and manipulation, as well as education and exercise training. If your doctor prescribes physiotherapy for you, ask him exactly what sort of treatment he is prescribing and what he expects it to achieve.

Question: How long is back pain likely to last?

Answer: There is no way to tell for sure. Each attack is a result of a number of separate factors, and the duration will depend on the degree of wear, the response to treatment, and your attitude, among other things. Separate acute attacks may run together, giving the impression of one continuous episode. As a general rule, however, a single attack of pain from a worn facet joint usually lasts from a few days to two weeks. Disc pain usually lasts from six weeks to three months.

Question: Should I let my doctor X-ray me whenever he wants to, or is there some limit I should impose?

Answer: In the amounts medical doctors use them, and with today's sophisticated techniques, X-rays are safe. As long as your doctor knows how many X-rays you have had, you can trust him not to overdo this valuable method of spinal examination.

Question: What is the difference between a doctor, a chiropractor, and an osteopath?

Answer: A medical doctor holds a degree in medicine from a recognized medical school. Generally his course is a four-year program following university, with an additional year of internship, a sort of apprentice period.

An osteopath is also trained in a four-year program which includes many of the same elements as the standard medical-school curriculum. Schools of osteopathic medicine are located mainly in the United States, particularly in the eastern and southern states. The name osteopath suggests that these practitioners treat only diseases of the bone. In fact, they treat a wide range of medical problems, such as diabetes and high blood pressure. Osteopaths, like medical doctors, may attend post-graduate programs for training in surgery. Spinal surgery may be performed by either a medical doctor or an osteopath.

Chiropractors are trained in a four-year program which stresses spinal anatomy and manipulation of the spine. Their expertise is much more limited than that of the doctor or the osteopath, and their treatments are related exclusively to problems that can be resolved by manipulation.

Question: Whenever I have an acute attack of back pain, the left side of my back swells up. What's going on?

Answer: What you feel is not swelling in the true sense; that is, it is not a collection of fluid under the skin. Your pain has caused your back to become very tight, and when the muscle is contracted it appears to swell. Although this is an involuntary action, it is otherwise the same as the muscular action that occurs in your upper arms when you strike the classic "strong man" pose by contracting your biceps. That is the likeliest explanation. Another possibility is that during that muscle spasm — a common response to back pain — your body is pulled over to one side. This posture causes you to stick one hip out, creating the impression that something has swollen up or "gone out of place."

Question: My doctor told me my problem is fibrositis. What is it?

Answer: The term fibrositis refers to small, painful nodules or lumps that develop under the skin. They are found most commonly in the low back or in the neck or across the top of the shoulders. The lumps are a secondary condition and are thought to reflect areas of painful muscle tension. Certainly they are quite painful if they are pushed or squeezed. Fibrositis has never been shown to be a separate or primary condition; most doctors believe it is the result rather than the cause of some other problem. For example, when a nerve in the back is irritated by reason of a worn facet joint or a protruding disc, the area of the body supplied by that nerve may develop these painful lumps. The exact nature of fibrositic nodules is puzzling; many surgeons have operated to remove the lumps, but when the skin has been opened, nothing has been found.

Your doctor may recommend that you have the lumps injected with a local anesthetic or cortisone. This can be quite effective in resolving the immediate problem. Even acupuncture needles inserted into these nodules can provide excellent pain relief. Unfortunately, however, all such injections deal only with the result of a basic problem, not the primary cause, and the pain relief is therefore often temporary. Even so, if you're the one who is in pain, you probably regard temporary relief as better than no relief at all. To achieve a more lasting solution, you will need treatment for the primary condition.

Question: What are the most important points for me to remember, as a backache victim?

Answer: It would even pay you to memorize these:
— Back pain is not a disease and therefore it has no cure. But it can be controlled.
— Your pain is real — not just in your head.
— Emotional upsets can increase your pain.
— Some days will be better than others.
— With rest, your acute attack will subside.
— Back exercise is good — unless it hurts.
— "Hurt" and "harm" are not always the same thing.
— To make your back better, you need to spend the time, you need to have the patience, and you need to accept the responsibility.

Index

ABOUT THE AUTHOR

HAMILTON HALL, M.D., F.R.C.S.(C), is an internation-
ally recognized authority on the treatment of back
pain. Dr. Hall is on the staff of Toronto General Hospital and Women's College Hospital (Toronto), is an
assistant professor at the University of Toronto, and
a member of the Canadian Orthopedic Association
and of the International Society for the Study of the
Lumbar Spine, a worldwide medical society limited
to 150 invited specialists.

In 1974, Dr. Hall founded the Canadian Back Education Units, a non-profit organization designed to
educate numbers of backache victims in the proper
care of their bad backs. The success and popularity
of his self-help program has spread rapidly; today
Back Education Units are active in major centres in
Canada, in Florida, Ohio, Kentucky, Michigan, and
Arizona, and in Perth, Australia.